LES GERMAINS
DIE GERMANEN
THE GERMANIC PEOPLES

DATE DUE			

JAPAN	Vadime Elisseeff, Curator at the Cernuschi Museum, Paris
MESOPOTAMIA	Jean-Claude Margueron, Member of the French Institute of Archaeology, Beirut
MEXICO	Jacques Soustelle
PERSIA I (From the origins to the Achaemenids)	Jean-Louis Huot, Member of the French Institute of Archaeology, Beirut
PERSIA II (From the Seleucids to the Sassanids)	Vladimir G. Lukonin, Head of the Oriental Department, Hermitage Museum, Leningrad
PERU	†Rafael Larco Hoyle, Director of the Rafael Larco Herrera Museum, Lima
PREHISTORY	
ROMANIA	Constantin Daicoviciu, Director of the Archaeological Institute of Cluj, and Emil Condurachi, Director of the Archaeological Institute of Bucarest
ROME	Gilbert Picard, Professor at the Sorbonne, Paris
SOUTHERN CAUCASUS	Boris B. Piotrovsky, Director of the Hermitage Museum, Leningrad
SOUTHERN SIBERIA	Mikhail Gryaznov, Professor at the Archaeological Institute, Leningrad
SYRIA-PALESTINE I (Ancient Orient)	Jean Perrot, Head of the French Archaeological Mission in Israel
SYRIA-PALESTINE II (Classical Orient)	Michael Avi Yonah, Professor at the University of Jerusalem, and David Ussishkin of the University of Jerusalem
THAILANDE	M.C. Sudhadradis Diskul, Professor at the Silpakorn University, Bangkok
TRANSHIMALAYA	Giuseppe Tucci, President of the Italian Institute for the Middle and Far East, Rome
URARTU	Boris B. Piotrovsky, Director of the Hermitage Museum, Leningrad

ARCHAEOLOGIA MVNDI

Series prepared under the direction of
Jean Marcadé, Professor of Archaeology
at the University of Bordeaux

ROLF HACHMANN

THE GERMANIC PEOPLES

Translated from the German by James Hogarth

37 illustrations in colour, 120 in black and white

NAGEL PUBLISHERS, GENEVA . PARIS . MUNICH

© 1971 by NAGEL PUBLISHERS, GENEVA (SWITZERLAND)

Printed in Switzerland

CONTENTS

PREFACE

*O*n the map of world archaeology the Germanic domain is, if not a terra incognita, at any rate an area whose boundaries vary with the particular period considered and the particular yardstick applied.

The first of the problems presented by Germanic archaeology, and one central to all the others, is that of defining the field. It is a matter not so much of seeking new sources of information as of making the best use of the texts and documents already available. The methods of Germanic archaeology are of two kinds: a critical approach is necessary for the interpretation of the written sources, technical skills are required for classifying and understanding the material remains of a mode of life and thought which is so far removed from our own. The results do not take the form of spectacular resurrections of a splendid past or the revelation and illumination of wide-ranging historical perspectives, but rather of the patient investigation and progressive comprehension of a culture. In this quest the archaeologist achieves a gradual insight into the economic and social systems of the Germanic peoples, their tribal and religious organisation, their mental concepts and their religious beliefs. And as for their art and architecture, although they left no major architectural monuments they did produce a wide variety of original and interesting work—as the reader can judge from the illustrations in this book, in which Professor Hachmann gives a careful and authoritative account of the present state of archaeological research.

J. M.

THE PROBLEMS

I

*"But since we can have no full knowledge of the ancient German nation
(Plate 1) we must take care not to lose the little we know and the
few remains it has left to us, but must bring them together and hold them
in honour; for this is a matter which concerns the honour of our land and
our forefathers who dwelt therein a thousand or it may be two thousand
years ago, who were our progenitors through many intervening generations
and who with much travail cultivated and made fruitful the soil which they
had found waste and desolate."*

Sebastian Münster, Cosmographia Universalis, *Basle, 1544*.

The Problem of Germanic Identity

Who were the Germanic peoples? The reader may be perplexed to find the question asked at the outset of this study. Need it be asked at all, he may wonder? Has it any real meaning? Clearly these doubts must be resolved before we go any farther.

At first sight, of course, the question seems to answer itself. But is this really so? Is this a purely rhetorical question—one which suggests its own answer, which does not need to be answered directly, and which therefore ought not even to be asked? Or is it, perhaps, a question to which there *is* no answer, and which again is better not asked?

Who were, then, the Germanic peoples? The forefathers of the present-day Germans? An alien and barbarous northern race? The conquerors of Britain? The creators of mediaeval Western culture? The destroyers of Rome and of the whole ancient world? What a variety of answers are possible in the light of our present knowledge! The ordinary informed observer may perhaps feel drawn towards one or other of the many possible answers, and then on reflection may hesitate: should he not first hear what the experts have to say—philologists, historians, archaeologists, students of religion and all the other specialists who may have something to contribute?

Here again the enquirer may find it difficult to get a clear answer. He may be told by the philologist, for example, that the Germanic peoples were a population group who spoke Germanic languages or dialects. This includes the Goths, the Franks and the Alamanni, no doubt; but what about the Marcomanni, the Ubii, the Vangiones, the Cherusci? And how much do we know, anyway, about the language spoken by the Ubii?

The historians for their part may apply the name Germanic to a group of peoples who for many centuries represented a recurring military threat to the Roman Empire and in the end destroyed it—or at any rate its western half. The first to appear were the Cimbri and Teutoni, followed by the Cherusci and Marcomanni, and finally by the Goths, Vandals and Franks. But then we are faced with another question: were the Teutoni in fact a Germanic people at all?

Or are the Germanic peoples to be identified as a group sharing the same religious conceptions—the cult of Nerthus, the sacred grove of the Semnones, the shrine of the goddess Tanfana; the Aesir and Vanir, Tiu, Wodan and Donar? But here we are under the difficulty that we do not know when the Germanic peoples first began to worship Wodan, the god known in Nordic mythology as Odin.

At this stage of our enquiry, therefore, we must turn to the archaeologists for an answer. But perhaps before doing so we should reformulate our original question. Instead of asking who were the Germanic peoples as a group, should we not rather seek to identify the various peoples included within that group?

What, then, can we learn from the archaeological evidence—from the graves and burial grounds, the hoards of precious objects, the settlement sites? In particular, what information can we glean from the jewellery, the tools and the weapons recovered by excavation? What, we may enquire, is the typical Germanic weapon, and why did it become so? The archaeologists tell us that Germanic warriors used the Celtic long sword and later the Roman short sword or *gladius*; but what about the *spatha* and the sax, the bow and arrow, the battle-axe, the francisc or throwing-axe? When did they become Germanic weapons? Here again we are faced with problems. And archaeologists, not being philologists, get no direct help from the Germanic language—even supposing that such a language existed. Can they, then, look for aid to Germanic history? But is it not part of Roman history and thus the concern of the ancient historian? And who, in any event, are the particular Germanic peoples with whom the archaeologist is—or ought to be—concerned? The Germans of the present day speak a Germanic tongue; or so at any rate the philologists assure us. But if this is so why do we put our question in the past tense: who *were* the Germans? They still seem to exist today, so that our question should rather be: who *are* the Germans? No, we must try again; this is still not the right question.

Is all this merely sophistry—mere trifling with words—or is it helping us to feel our way towards a definition of our subject: one of which most people know little and with which fewer still have seriously concerned themselves? Have we strayed into a labyrinth from which there is no issue? The Germanic peoples present a problem; but it is one which is usually—perhaps deliberately—ignored. In our perplexity perhaps only one thing is clear: that the question "Who were the Germanic peoples?" is a perfectly proper one, but that there is a heavy emphasis on the interrogative *who*. In this simple question all the problems of Germanic studies—problems of language, culture, religion and history—are comprehended; and for its answer we must look hopefully to the archaeologist as one among a group of specialists concerned with the study of the Germanic peoples.

But we are not yet ready to consider the archaeological evidence. Before tackling the complex problems which it presents we must seek to clear up the confusion of words and terminology with which we are beset.

Problems of Terminology

The *Chronicle of the Origin, Descent and Achievements of the Ancient Germans ("Chronica... der vralten Teutschen")*, written in 1541 by Johannes Aventinus, the "Bavarian Herodotus", was one of the first works to identify the *Teutsche* (or modern *Deutsche*) with the ancient Germans *(Germanen)*. Aventinus recognised that the ancient Germans were the ancestors of the Germans of his own day: a fact which had not previously been distinctly realised. Henceforth, in the literature of German humanism and in later periods, the two terms, *Deutsche* and *Germanen*, were regarded as synonymous.

This equivalence was accepted for more than three centuries. As late as 1837 Kaspar Zeuss gave the title *Die Deutschen und die Nachbarstämme* ("The Germans and their Neighbours") to his study of the ethnography of northern, central and eastern Europe in ancient times, a work which was to achieve a considerable reputation; and in 1848 Jacob Grimm wrote a *Geschichte der deutschen Sprache* ("History of the German Language") dealing with the history of the Germanic languages. It was not until the latter part of the 19th century that *Deutsche* and *Germanen* were once again distinguished in German scholarly usage. There remained a residual uncertainty about the point of time at which it ceased to be right to refer to *Germanen* and became appropriate to talk of *Deutsche*. Nor, of course, was it clearly established when the first identifiable *Germanen* had appeared on the scene.

Outside the German language area there were some variations in terminology. Thus in English usage the word "Dutch", derived from the Old High

14

German *diutisk* (modern German *deutsch*), became restricted to the language and people of the Netherlands (including West Friesland), and it became necessary to find a new name for the *Deutsche*. Here again the humanistic equivalence between *Teutsche* and *Germanen* came into play, and henceforth the modern inhabitants of Germany were known as Germans. This in turn created a need for a new name to identify the ancient *Germanen*, who accordingly were called Teutons—after the name of a tribe who were in all probability not themselves of Germanic stock. Here again we find a confusion of terminology.

In Old French the adjective *tieis* and the proper name *Tiedeis*, applied to the people—corresponding to the Old High German *diutisk*—are occasionally found. These terms did not, however, become generally accepted, and in their place the Germans became known in the French language as *Allemands*, after the name of the Germanic tribe living nearest to French-speaking territory, the Alamanni. The ancient *Germanen* then became *Germains*. But closer examination shows that the line of demarcation between *Germains* and *Allemands* is not precisely defined, and does not correspond exactly with the distinction between *Germanen* and *Deutsche*. The terms *Germains* and *Germanen* are thus not completely equivalent.

Native speakers of the various languages are not fully conscious of these differences of usage. It is, of course, perfectly easy to see how they came about: partly on the basis of scholarly (or pseudo-scholarly) interpretations, partly as a result of unconscious and quite spontaneous semantic changes.

If, however—for convenience of argument—we take *Germanen* and *Germains*, Teutons and ancient Germans, as basically identical conceptions we are not much farther forward. We are still left with the problem of deciding who these ancient Germans were. There are at least three possible answers to this question, with still other possibilities discernible in the background. Properly speaking, "Germanic" is primarily a linguistic term designating a group of languages which show close affinities with one another—English, Dutch and Afrikaans, Frisian, Danish, Norwegian, Swedish and German. The kinship of these languages is indisputable and generally accepted; but why, it may well be asked, are they all known as Germanic? It cannot even be claimed that any one of the peoples concerned ever referred to itself, of its own accord and without any scholarly intervention, as Germanic.

The term comes from the Germani, a people who lived on the borders of the Roman Empire beyond the Rhine-Danube frontier. This people, it is suggested, must have spoken "Germanic"; but what evidence have we of this? Only two things are clear. The first is that we have practically no remains, during the first three centuries of our era, of the language of the Germani who are mentioned in the ancient authors. The few "Germanic" personal names tell us little about the language, the few recorded words even less. Moreover the names cannot always be distinguished with any certainty from "Celtic" names: thus the "Germanic" ruler Ariovistus, leader of the Suebi, Marcomanni, Vangiones, Triboci, Nemetes, Sedusii and Harudes, with whom Caesar had to contend in the first year of the Gallic War, has a counterpart in a British oculist bearing the same name. The second established fact is that not one of the numerous Romans who came into contact with the Germani was able to understand, still less to speak, the language of any Germanic tribe. In all their dealings with "Germani" the Romans had to depend on the services of interpreters, except where the people they came into contact with themselves spoke Latin.

To these two considerations a third may be added. The peoples whom the Romans called Germani did not apply this name to themselves: indeed they had no single term comprehending all "Germani". They had no consciousness of any "Germanic" ethnic community, recognising only a variety of separate tribes, large or small; and in referring to themselves they used the tribal name.

❧ TABVLA EVROPÅE IIII·

Oceanus Germanicus

Alociæ infulæ

SCANDIA MAIOR

DACIA

Cimbri

Scandiæ minores infulæ

Saxones infulæ

Phundusi

Charudes

Chali

Cobandi

Sabalingi

Sigulones

Saxones

Cimbrica Cherfone sui

Lethurgui

Pharo dyni

Teuroroari

Virunum

Tauroncæ

Sadini

Rugini

Virunu

Businum

Ruricli

Aluponcs

Occanus Sarmaticus

Cauchi maiores

Cauchi parui

Angriuari

Lancobardi

Dulgumni

Marionis

Viruni

Aucrpi

Diduni

Omini

Longi

Lun

Bun

Lingæ
Calucones

Batini

Corconti

Bonocheros

Salono

Camani

Cheruf

Sycambri

Langobardi

Sulebi

Tingeri

Ingriones

Innuergi

Vargiones

Carithni
Vilpl

GER · R · MANIA

MAGNA

Cafuari

Charte

Melibocus mons

Tubanti

Vu burgi

Cogni

Chaite

Teuriochema

Hercynia filua

Turoni

Marungi

Cunones

Chruon

Vanfu

Gabreta fylua

Luna fylua

SARMATIAE
EVROPÆ
PARS

Marcomani

Sudeni

Bemi

Eluccoru heremus

Parma campi

Ars Flauia

Alaemonis

Adrabæ campi

Rauracæ

Tilacatæ

Vibiū

Dacirum

Rhetiæ pars

Vindeliciæ pars

Norici pars

Pannoniæ fuperioris pars

Pannoniæ inferioris pars

GERMANIAE ciuitates.
Aftuia, Alifos, Afcancalis, Afcaburgum, Argeo
lia, Arfonium, Alifum, arficua, Afanca, Abilano
um, Arduum, Bonitium, Bogadium, Budori
gum, Cergum, Bicurgium, Credelita, Camo
rauum, Candunum, Colocaeuon, Cambochis, Co
ridorgis, Eclamana. Dunona. Eburon
Graueonarum Hegemonia. Leuphana, Lu
ruuero, Logiduni, Lomofaleum, Leucariftu.
Mamitium, Mefunum, Mattiacum, Mefocelou,
Menofgeda, Marobudi, Melodunum, Medela
Lemon. Naudia, Neomeriuon, Noefum.
Phrifia, Phurgifati, Parienna, Phcegarum,
Phabiranum. Rugium, Rufiana, Rhobodani
Iragone, Setuacotum, Setua, Steruonta, Seu
godunum, Setidaua, Stragona, Sufudata, Sierr
montum, Scurgum, Sciuicunda. Treelia, Tru
na, Tulifurgr. B, Tulipharduni, Trophae Dru
fi, Terodunum. Vfbalim, Virunum, Virunum.
Reliqua loca in tabula funt expreffa.

Paralf 19

Paralf 18

Paralf 17

Paralf 16

Paralf 15

1

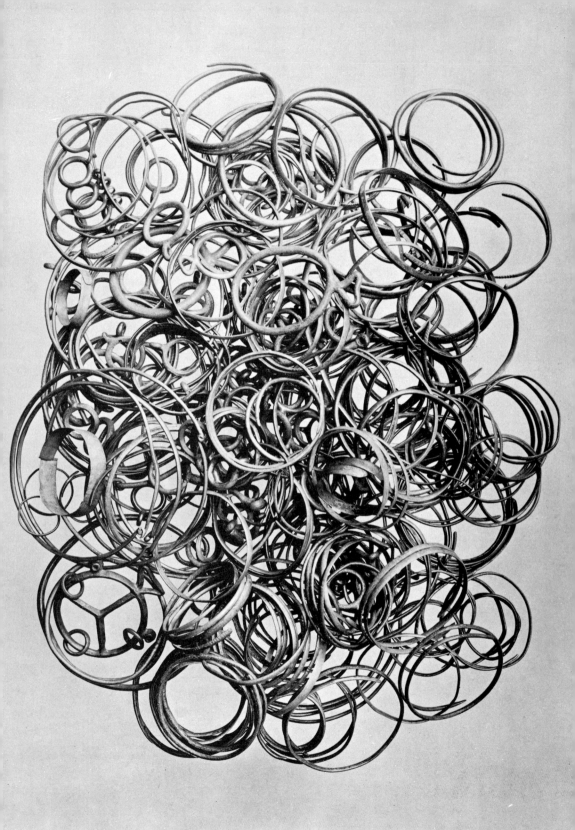

3

4

← 2

5

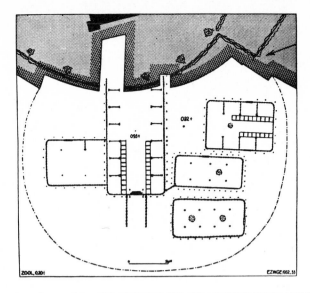

6

7

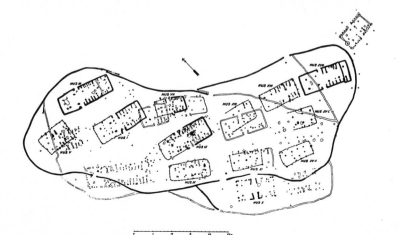

8

11

12

13

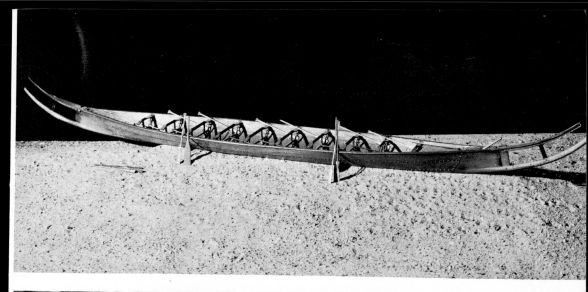

14,15

16   17

What justification have we, therefore, for calling the Germanic languages Germanic? In fact we have none, apart from the tacit assumption that those peoples whom the Romans called Germani all spoke the same language, though in a variety of dialects. This unspoken agreement rests on the belief that the names given to peoples of non-Roman and non-Greek stock in ancient times were determined on the same principles as in our own day. The validity of this assumption is open to question. In terms of Greek and Roman ideas of ethnography, who were the Germani? What did the Romans mean by a German? The answer to this question is central to our whole enquiry.

We must, however, delay the answer for a little; for there is a fourth point to be considered. In late antiquity the term Germani fell out of general use, becoming a purely literary term used by poets and scholars in the sense in which they found it employed in older writers. In accounts of contemporary events the word Germani was not used, being replaced by a new collective term, *barbari*, the "barbarians". This word, however, had long had a different and wider connotation, being applied also to peoples who had never been known as Germani—the Sarmatians, Huns, Alans, etc. The individual tribes were also designated by their own distinctive names—Goths, Vandals, Gepidae and so on. The Franks and Alamanni, however, were still sometimes called Germani, and by a curious circumstance the old Roman province of Gaul was occasionally referred to as Germania, being ruled by the Franks, who were also known as Germani.

In this later period, from the 4th century onwards, the surviving literary evidence becomes rather more plentiful. To this period belong the translation of the Bible by the Gothic bishop Ulfilas and the earliest runic inscriptions. These are the oldest of the documents which have made it possible to build up a picture of the development of the Germanic languages. It is certain that the languages of the Goths, the Alamanni and Franks, the Anglo-Saxons and the Scandinavian peoples were related. Of the relationship of these languages to the languages of the Vangiones, the Ubii, the Sugambri, the Cherusci and Cimbri, the Teutoni and the Ambrones, however, we know little or nothing; and there is no ground for believing that these peoples too spoke Germanic dialects, merely because the Romans were accustomed to refer to them as Germani.

Clearly, therefore, the term Germanic as used by modern philologists and the apparently similar term employed in ancient times in fact express very different conceptions. The archaeologist's use of the term need not necessarily coincide with the philologist's. Indeed it cannot so coincide, unless we are prepared to postulate that wherever there is a Germanic language there must of necessity be a Germanic culture; and a number of historical examples can be cited against any such proposition. Nor can the archaeologist's definition of the term Germanic be identical with that accepted in ancient times.

What follows from all this? Are we to find at the end of our quest that the concept of the Germanic peoples has suddenly vanished into thin air, that it is a mere will o' the wisp with no foundation in fact? But what in fact do we know of the culture of those peoples who, according to the findings of modern linguistic study, spoke Germanic languages or dialects? It is well known, of course, that a people's language itself gives much information about their culture, so that linguistic history can make a contribution to cultural history. In their form as well as their content, linguistic documents often provide evidence on a people's culture. We must therefore enquire what the linguistic evidence tells us about the diffusion of Germanic culture.

We do, of course, know a good deal about the culture of those peoples whom the Romans called Germani, including those of whose language we know nothing. The remains of their material culture have been preserved in the soil and in due time recovered by archaeologists. At once, however, we are struck by the fact that the culture of the peoples who were known to the

Romans as Germani and lived on the right bank of the Rhine in the period before the birth of Christ was similar to that of the peoples on the left bank whom the Romans called Gauls. Can we resolve this paradox? Is there any population group which we can define as Germanic without coming up against a difficulty of this kind?

Evidently our original question, "Who were the Germanic peoples?", was too optimistic: we must begin more cautiously and enquire whether there were any peoples who can properly be called Germanic at all.

The concept of the Germanic peoples comes to us from the ancient world. In the pursuit of our enquiry, therefore, we must now turn to Rome and Greece and to the Greco-Roman world. Here we shall find the answer to much—indeed almost all—that has been perplexing us.

The Germanic Peoples in the Ancient World

In the year 113 B.C. disturbing news reached Rome from the north. The Republic's northern frontier, which since the defeat of the Celts in Upper Italy had been regarded as secure, seemed again to be threatened. A tribe of whom nothing had previously been heard, the Cimbri, had burst into Noricum in the eastern Alpine region and inflicted a sharp defeat on the consul responsible for these northern territories, Papirius Carbo. The way into Italy seemed open to the victors. The Cimbri did not, however, take advantage of this opportunity—of which they were probably not aware—but turned back through southern Germany and appeared in southern Gaul in 109 B.C., now accompanied by the Teutoni. A number of indecisive battles were fought, and then in 105 a large Roman army suffered an annihilating defeat at Arausio (Orange). There was now nothing to stop the Cimbri and Teutoni from making straight for Italy and marching on Rome; but instead of doing so they split up, the Cimbri heading for Spain and the Teutoni remaining in Gaul. A few years later the Cimbri returned from Spain and the two tribes joined up again. Soon, however, they went their separate ways once more: the Teutoni now set out to advance direct on Italy, while the Cimbri turned east, passed through southern Germany again, and then also made their way into Italy through the Alpine passes.

Meanwhile the consul Marius had reorganised the Roman army and recruited fresh forces. Taking advantage of the separation of the two tribes, he defeated the Teutoni at Aquae Sextiae (Aix-en-Provence) in the southern Rhône valley in 102 and the Cimbri, who had already reached the plain of the Po, at Vercellae (Vercelli) in the following year. The Cimbri and Teutoni were annihilated. The threat to Italy was averted for several generations, but the mortal danger which had loomed over Rome was not soon to be forgotten.

Where did they come from, these barbarian hordes who had brought Rome into such jeopardy? This was the question which exercised men's minds. The first person of any scholarly competence to express a view seems to have been the geographer Artemidorus of Ephesus, who, writing about the turn of the century, held the Cimbri to be Celts. Another scholar whose name is unknown to us believed them to be Celto-Scythians. Posidonius of Apamea, the leading Greek scholar of his day, spent some time in Rome and Massilia (Marseilles) in the last decade of the 1st century for the purpose of gathering information about the Cimbri and Teutoni. The conclusion of his investigations and of the shrewd reasoning which he based on them was that nothing was known, or could be known, about the origins of the Cimbri. The territories they had traversed in their wanderings were, he suggested, much too extensive, and their original homeland accordingly much too far away, for any information about them to have reached other peoples in the earlier period during which they had had no intercourse with the rest of the world. He was able to glean rather more information about the Teutoni. They and the Tigurini, who had accompanied them in their travels, were, he thought, two out of the three tribes in the Helvetic group, who had been attracted to join up with the Cimbri by the great quantities of booty from the eastern Alpine region which they carried with them on their passage through southern Germany. The homeland of the Teutoni must, therefore, have been within the area occupied by the Helvetii: that is, in southern Germany. Neither the Cimbri nor the Teutoni were referred to by Posidonius as Germani. Until his time the name of this people was totally unknown in the Roman Empire, and Posidonius himself heard it for the first time during his stay in Gaul. They were said to live on the Rhine, and Posidonius believed them to be Celts.

Too much importance need not, however, be attached to this classification, which reflected the peculiarities of Greek ethnographical nomenclature. As early as the 5th century B.C. Greek science had arrived at a firm view of the distribution of the various peoples throughout the world. In this view the regions in the far north-west, outside the Mediterranean area, were occupied by the Celts, those in the far north-east by the Scythians. It followed, therefore, that any new population group discovered in the north-west must be Celts, any group in the north-east Scythians. Only in the intermediate region, it was believed, could there sometimes be mixed populations, and to such hybrid stocks the designation of Celto-Scythians was applied. Accordingly the Cimbri and Teutoni were described as Celts because they had first become known to the Greeks in the far north-west. On the other hand the label of Celto-Scythians which was also applied to them reflected the belief that they must originally have come from the frontier region where Celts and Scythians met and mingled. Both designations were evidently mere conventional terms serving to disguise the fact that nothing was really known at all about the origins of these peoples.

As the earliest information we have about the Cimbri and Teutoni, Posidonius's remarks have greater weight than most of the statements by later authors; but their value is still further enhanced by the trouble which he took to collect the relevant data, showing a zeal which was quite exceptional before his time and was only rarely displayed by later writers of antiquity. He spent some time in Massilia and visted the battlefield of Aquae Sextiae, and must have travelled as far afield as the Rhineland in pursuit of his enquiries. As the guest of Massiliote Greeks and Celtic princes he had access to information such as was enjoyed by no one else either before or after his time. He was able to speak to witnesses who had lived through the wars with the Cimbri, and to people who had came into direct contact with both Cimbri and Teutoni.

Accordingly when we find Posidonius regarding the Teutoni as Helvetii (i.e. as Celts) and note that he did not know the exact origin of the Cimbri but certainly did not consider them to be Germani—although he knew of the Germani as a people of Celtic stock—we are puzzled to know what led the ancients to suppose that the Cimbri and Teutoni were Germanic peoples.

The statement that the Cimbri and Teutoni were Germanic is found for the first time in Caesar, who was also the first to give a detailed account of the Germani and to identify them as a population group distinct from the Celts. These two statements—that the Cimbri and Teutoni were Germanic peoples, and that the Germani were distinct from the Celts—are closely connected, and both statements reflect Caesar's own purposes and military objectives.

After his victory over the Helvetii in the first year of the Gallic War (58 B.C.) Caesar learned from the Haedui, one of the largest Gallic tribes, that other Gallic tribes had recruited Germanic troops as mercenaries. Originally, he was told, only a small group of these Germanic warriors had crossed the Rhine, but later they had come in large numbers and established themselves in Gaul; their king was named Ariovistus.

In his references to the Germanic forces led by Ariovistus Caesar frequently takes occasion, directly or indirectly, to stress the function of the Rhine as an ethnic boundary between Gauls and Germans. This suggests at first sight that he had precise and reliable information about the population living on both banks of the Rhine; but if we consider the sources available to him—including the direct information he obtained from the interrogation of prisoners and the indirect information supplied by Gallic informants—we must conclude that in this first year of the war he was not particularly well informed.

It is evident, on the other hand, that even in the first year of the war he was pursuing specific political and military objectives. He made great play with his desire to free the Gallic tribes from alien oppression, and accordingly began by defeating first the Helvetii and then the hordes led by Ariovistus; but in reality he set out deliberately to counter any influence from outside Gaul so that he might assert his own influence the more firmly and decisively. The events of the second year of the war threw further light on his intentions, making it clear that the Rhine played an important part in his military plans and his war aims.

Caesar had come to Gaul, as later events showed beyond doubt, to establish a firm base for the political rôle which he hoped to play at Rome. It was important, of course, that these plans should not become known at Rome; but suspicions had already been aroused, and this made it all the more necessary for Caesar to conceal his true intention with the greatest care. The task entrusted to him was to pacify Gaul, and he contrived with great skill to make the most of the responsibility imposed on him, shrewdly playing down his own personal part in events. He could afford to let these events speak for themselves. Idolised by his troops, with a trained and battle-hardened army behind him, he rose slowly but surely to supreme power, apparently without any effort on his own part. All his actions seemed to follow inevitably from the circumstances. All that he did was based on careful calculation, but his own account suggested that he was forced by events to do it, almost despite himself. After originally showing some disposition in his favour the Celts opposed his policy of pacification: their resistance, therefore, had to be broken. The Germanic tribes on the far bank of the Rhine were always potential allies of the rebellious Celts, and moreover—as Ariovistus had shown—were avid for power and set on expansion; in both respects they represented an obstacle to Caesar's work of pacification. This at any rate was the light in which Caesar presented the situation.

In fact Caesar very soon realised that the Rhine was the boundary of any military expansion to the north: not only the natural boundary but also the necessary boundary. Since he was commissioned to pacify the Gallic tribes, the territory up to the Rhine must be occupied by Gauls, and the land beyond it must be a different country occupied by a different people. This was why Caesar constantly stressed the function of the Rhine as a boundary between the Germanic and Gallic peoples. The Germani interested him only to the extent that they disturbed the Rhine frontier. All his military activities can be understood as a reflection of these ideas. In this sense, therefore, the Germanic peoples were almost a political invention of Caesar's: almost, but not wholly.

Thus the Germanic peoples originally came into prominence to serve Caesar's own political ends. He deliberately built them up as a non-Gallic population group on the right bank of the Rhine who were constantly disturbing the peace of Gaul.

What did Caesar really know of ethnographical conditions on the Rhine? That is the question we must now consider. How much could he have known when, after six years' campaigning in Gaul, he wrote his famous ethnographic account of the Germanic peoples in 53 B.C.? It might be thought that during these years he had ample opportunities to assemble an abundance of observations; but what in fact he produced was a mixture of traditional ideas about the culture of the nomadic peoples who were believed to live to the east of the Celts—the Scythians of Greek ethnography—and of miscella-

22

23

24

26

25

27 →

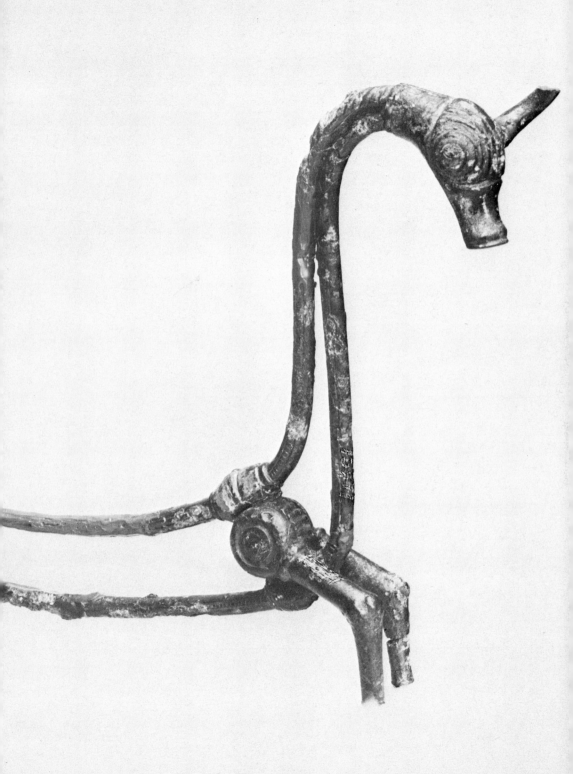

28

29

30

31

32

33

34

neous information from a variety of sources, some of them of very questionable reliability, in which truth was mingled with evident invention and sheer mendacity.

What can Caesar have known of the languages of the Gallic and Germanic peoples on the Rhine? He begins his first book with the well known and lapidary statement that Gaul was divided into three parts, occupied by the Belgae, the Aquitani and the Galli or Gauls after whom the whole country was named. He notes that the three peoples differed in language, institutions and laws. Of the language of the Germanic peoples, however, he tells us nothing. Can it be that he knew nothing about it? Surely, for the most obvious military reasons, the Romans must have devoted intensive effort to reconnoitring geographical and ethnographical conditions in territory occupied by their enemies or potential enemies? And surely for the purpose of such reconnaissance it was necessary for even the lower command levels to be familiar with the languages spoken in the area? What evidence is there to show that the Romans did *not* have regard to the language and name of a tribe in determining whether it was Germanic or not? Matters of this kind are of such importance for military and political purposes that those responsible could surely not be content with accepted commonplaces and unchecked reports?

We know that the Romans and Greeks took a great interest in their own languages. Their linguistic concepts, however, were very different from those of our own day: the relationships between different languages as they have been established by modern comparative philology were beyond their ken, even within their own languages. It was, of course, known that languages other than Latin and Greek were spoken in the Roman Empire, but these languages were not considered worthy of scholarly study. There was an equal lack of interest in the languages of the barbarians outside the Empire. No attempt was made to learn these languages, apart from a few individual words, since it was expected that the other peoples would learn Latin or Greek. The Romans depended on interpreters when required, or on anyone else who could help to establish communication. To them the particular languages spoken by enemies or subject peoples were not of any military or political importance.

For Caesar the Rhine was the boundary between the geographical areas of Germania and Gallia, and the Germani were the inhabitants of Germania. In this respect linguistic conditions were of no significance. No Roman—not even Caesar himself—would ever have enquired whether the Germanic peoples all spoke the same language or what that language was. To them the Germani were, quite simply, the people who lived on the right bank of the Rhine.

Strangely at variance with Caesar's emphasis on the Rhine as the boundary between the Gallic and Germanic peoples is his statement that there were also Germani settled on the west bank of the river, in northern Gaul. Among these Germanic tribes on the left bank he included the Eburones, Condrusi, Paemani, Caeroesi and Segni, and also—on account of their pretended descent from the Cimbri—the Aduatuci, whom he also included among the Belgae. The information he gives about the Belgae themselves, however, is obscure and contradictory. He describes them as Gauls, in the wider sense of the term; but he also records a statement by emissaries of the Belgic Remi that most of the Belgae were of Germanic origin and had crossed the Rhine into Gaul in earlier times.

The existence of Germanic tribes on the left bank of the Rhine raises a variety of problems and has been the subject of much discussion, which has not yet fully cleared up the difficulties. In this connection the following facts appear to be of particular significance. It was apparently only after Caesar had established his conception of the Germanic peoples that he learned of the presence of Germani on the west bank of the Rhine, in northern Gaul; for it is only in the book describing the second year of the Gallic War that he mentions the Germani in northern Gaul. Although the existence of these particular Germanic inhabitants destroyed the whole basis of his conception, he made no attempt to change it. No doubt the name of Germani had become so firmly attached to the tribes on the left bank that their existence could not be denied. It is notable also that Caesar puts the reference to the Germani on the left bank in the mouths of native informants.

Caesar was not the only author to mention the presence of Germani on the left bank of the Rhine. Barely half a century later the geographer Strabo noted that the Belgic Nervii regarded themselves as Germani; and a hundred years later Tacitus repeated the story of the Germanic origin of the Nervii, adding that the Treveri also claimed Germanic descent.

Both Caesar and Tacitus, in representing the Belgae and Treveri as of Germanic origin, had in mind the Germani on the east bank of the Rhine. It cannot now be established with certainty whether the Belgae and Treveri meant the same thing when they referred to themselves as Germani. We can no doubt assume, however, that their conception of Germanic nationality came closer to the facts of the situation than Caesar's.

In assessing the significance of the references to the Belgae and Treveri as Germanic, it must be borne in mind that the name is not recorded as being applied to themselves by any other tribes. In claiming Germanic origin, therefore, the Belgae and Treveri cannot have been thinking of the whole body of Germanic peoples in the sense in which Caesar uses the term. We thus have a rather shadowy picture of a group of tribes in northern Gaul who called themselves Germani and had some consciousness of racial solidarity.

Probably these were the Germani of whom Posidonius heard on his journey up the Rhône valley. They are also, of course, mentioned by Tacitus in a much discussed passage. The people who in his day were known as Tungri, he says, had originally been called Germani. It was only at a later stage that the name of Germani was extended to all the peoples on the right bank of the Rhine, who did not originally apply this name to themselves or perhaps even use it at all. It looks, therefore, as if Caesar himself was responsible for the wider use of the term.

From Strabo's account—probably based on Posidonius—we learn that there were also Germanic tribes living on the right bank of the Rhine. Caesar's conception of the Germani also makes it necessary to suppose that the old-established group of Germanic tribes in northern Gaul extended over the Rhine, for in the first year of the Gallic War he was still unaware of the existence of Germani in northern Gaul. There must have been one or more tribes on the right bank of the Rhine bearing the name of Germani, whose presence led him to describe all the tribes on the right bank as Germanic.

The ancient sources give us no clear picture of the ethnographical character of the original group of Germanic tribes. Posidonius regarded them as Celts, no doubt because most of them lived on the left bank of the Rhine, which he regarded as the boundary between Celts and Scythians—in a sense the continuation of the Danube frontier between the two peoples. He must have argued, therefore, that they were bound to be Celts because they lived on the left bank of the Rhine. Caesar regarded the same group of tribes as Germanic, however, merely because they were known as Germani.

The result of this survey of the ancient authors from Posidonius to Tacitus is surprising, on two counts. We have observed in the first place that the ancient accounts reveal the existence of a group of peoples living in northern Gaul and on the Rhine who called themselves Germani; and we have seen that Caesar transferred this name of Germani to the whole population living on the right bank of the Rhine, applying the name, without much concern for language or culture, to all the peoples of Germania, the region bounded on the west by Gallia and extending in the east to Sarmatia (the territory occupied by the Sarmatians, who were known to the Greeks as Scythians). The second significant fact is that Greek ethnography did not recognise the

Germani as an independent population group. To them the Germanic peoples were Celts when they were encountered in the west, Scythians when they lived in the east. This conception prevailed in Greek science right into the Byzantine period.

But the situation is further complicated by the change in the Roman conception of the Germanic peoples which took place in late antiquity. Germania now became a word used by poets and men of letters because they found it employed in older literature. The name was no longer used with reference to contemporary conditions; or, if it was, had a quite different meaning. The Goths, Gepidae, Vandals and all the other Germanic peoples living in the east were still referred to only by their tribal names, and the peoples living in the west were usually known as Alamanni and Franks; but when the term Germani was, exceptionally, applied in a contemporary context it meant the Alamanni and Franks. In this usage it might be applied to both peoples together or to one or other of them—most commonly to the Franks alone.

Thus our analysis of the term Germani has yielded five different interpretations. First, there were the Germani who lived in northern Gaul and on the Rhine, who applied the name to themselves and were so called by the "true" Gauls who lived to the south of them. Secondly, the Germani whom the Romans knew in the period around the birth of Christ and in the three following centuries as the inhabitants of Germania, the area to the east of the Rhine which was bounded on the west by Gallia and on the east by Sarmatia. Thirdly, the Germani who for most of the Greek authors writing in the centuries after the birth of Christ and late into the Byzantine period were part of the group of Celtic peoples living in north-western Europe. Fourthly, the Germani who were known to the Romans of late antiquity as the barbarians dwelling beyond the Rhine frontier: the Alamanni and more particularly the Franks. Fifthly, the Germani defined by modern scholars as a population group in central and northern Europe speaking Germanic languages or dialects.

At first sight, therefore, the results of our enquiry have not thrown much light on the problem which concerns us—particularly since there seems to be no evidence pointing towards one or other of these interpretations as the correct one. Certainly we can exclude the so-called Germani in northern Gaul, since a study of personal names, place names and the names of divinities shows with tolerable clarity that these tribes were not Germanic in the linguistic sense. We can also identify and appreciate the historical genesis of the Greek conception of the Germanic peoples. The age-old Greek ethnographic scheme, which recognised the existence in the north of no other peoples than Celts and Scythians, was never abandoned; and the Germani were therefore inevitably classified as Celts, or alternatively as Scythians when they lived to the north-east or sought to attack the Empire from that direction. The late Roman conception of the Germani can also be explained and understood in the light of history, representing as it did the narrowing down of an earlier connotation.

We are thus left with the question whether the earlier Roman conception of the Germanic peoples corresponded even approximately with the findings of modern linguistic scholarship. A complete equivalence is not to be expected, for there is no necessary match between the Roman view of the Germani as inhabitants of the region known as Germania and the modern definition of the Germanic peoples as a linguistic group. It may well have been the case, however, that all the inhabitants of Germania were Germanic in the sense that they spoke Germanic languages or dialects. This is surely the decisive question, the answer to which may throw light on our problem—if indeed the question can be answered at all. It will no doubt be agreed that at any rate some of the Germani known to the Romans spoke languages which could properly be classified as Germanic; but which of them? There were of course the Goths, then living on the right bank of the Vistula, into whose language Ulfilas translated the Bible in the 4th century. But were the Goths of the period around the birth of Christ the ancestors, in the full sense of the term, of the Goths of Ulfilas, of Alaric, of Theodoric? We cannot be sure. We do know that at the time they lived in southern France the Visi-goths still preserved some remnant of the ancient Gothic stock, as the legends of their origin indicate. Apart from this, however, we know only that the Goths absorbed a variety of alien racial elements during the vicissitudes of the 2nd, 3rd and 4th centuries and, to an even greater extent, in later periods. There may also have been a Germanic-speaking group among the Marco-manni, who after living for centuries in Bohemia made a home for themselves in southern Germany as the Bajuwari. But can the Bajuwari be regarded without further ado as the descendants of the Marcomanni?

And what are we to make of the Germanic tribes on the Rhine, the first peoples to be described by the Romans as Germanic? What do we know of the languages of the Ubii, the Sugambri, the Mattiaci, the Usipetes and Tencteri, the Vangiones, the Nemetes and Triboci? No remains of the lan-guages themselves have survived, and the few place names known seem to be non-Germanic. This is the sum total of our knowledge—at any rate if we confine ourselves to the demonstrable facts.

If, therefore, the evidence considered so far can take us no farther, may we look to archaeology to guide us on our way, to bring order out of confusion, to throw light in dark places, to lead us to a satisfactory definition of the people with whom we are concerned?

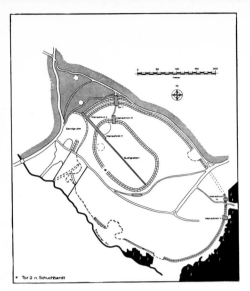

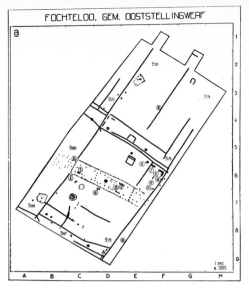

FOCHTELOO. GEM. OOSTSTELLINGWERF

36

37

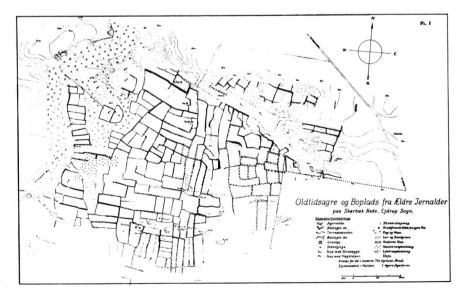

38

39

Oldtidsagre og Boplads fra Ældre Jernalder
paa Skørbæk Hede, Ejdrup Sogn.

40

41

42

43

47

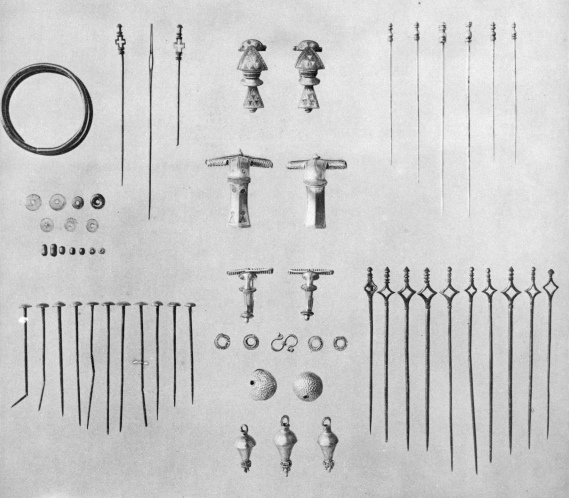

48,49

51

52

THE ARCHAEOLOGICAL EVIDENCE

II

The Germans on the Rhine

> "*It is no doubt generally admitted that the history of a country or people —
> that is, a coherent account of events and personalities arranged in chrono-
> logical order — cannot be conceived unless it be based on written historical
> material or (as the phrase goes) on direct sources; but neither is it in
> doubt that monuments and remains from early times, whether with a
> speaking voice or dumb, are rightly to be regarded as direct historical
> sources. Although such remains cannot acquaint us with new facts and
> cannot serve either to correct ancient records of the succession of rulers
> or to establish chronological determinations, they are nevertheless capable
> when collected and collated, of giving us a clearer conception of the religion
> and culture, the manners and many other aspects of the life of our fore-
> fathers.*"

C. J. Thomsen, Ledetraad for nordisk oldkyndighed, *Copenhagen, 1836.*

Who were the Germanic peoples? Until recently the archaeologists'
answer to this question was simple and straightforward: the name
Germanic was applied to all the archaeologically identifiable cultures which the Romans held to be Germanic. "Germanic" meant what had
always been known as Germanic, and there was no more to be said.

Accordingly archaeologists, seeking traces of the Cimbri and Teutoni, who
were indisputably Germanic—for had not Caesar and all later writers said
so?—believed they had found what they were looking for in a series of cremation burials dating from around 100 B.C. Cremation was, of course, particularly widespread in this northerly heartland of the Germanic peoples,
where there could be no room for doubt about their nationality. The scholars
who maintained this view so firmly, however, overlooked the fact that cremation burials also occurred in what was indubitably Celtic territory: the archaeological "proof" of the Germanic affiliation of the Cimbri and Teutoni was

thus an illusion. Even today there is no archaeological evidence on these tribes. This is hardly matter for surprise. Why should we expect to identify the Teutoni in this way, when Posidonius tells us they were Celts? How can we hope to find evidence of the presence of the Cimbri when we do not know where they came from or whether they were Germans at all?

Faced with the archaeological evidence discovered in the Rhineland, the learned world could not but be puzzled by the fact that the Celtic material of the 1st century B.C. found on the left bank of the river was so strikingly similar to the Germanic material found on the right bank as to be almost identical. From this observation the logical but erroneous conclusion was drawn that the Celts and Germans could not be distinguished from one another on the basis of the archaeological evidence. It might have been concluded with equal plausibility, however, that perhaps the statements of the ancient writers were not entirely to be relied upon. The question might be asked: were the Mattiaci, the Ubii and Sugambri, the Vangiones, the Nemetes and Triboci in fact Germans at all?

If archaeology is to achieve significant results it must avoid being led astray either by the conceptions of the ancient world, so different from those of our own day, or by the theories of the philologists, since archaeologists cannot as a rule directly apprehend linguistic categories in their material. It must not, on the other hand, proceed eclectically, picking out one particular feature as significant in demarcating a culture and rejecting others as irrelevant. One individual form is of little use in defining the diffusion of different cultural groups and the boundaries between them: it is necessary to consider the whole of a particular culture in so far as it can be identified in the archaeological material. No doubt the archaeological sources are deplorably fragmentary; but is this not equally true of our other sources for such early periods—the accounts of ancient writers, the linguistic evidence? The material recovered by excavation has the great advantage over other sources that it yields information about the fundamental structure of a culture. In the first place, of course, it provides evidence on certain aspects of the material culture of a people—their pottery, their metal implements, the construction of their houses. But it also reveals a great deal about their way of life and thought—their dress, their manner of fighting, their religious practices (particularly those concerning the cult of the dead), their social structure and their economy. With the help of evidence of this kind it should surely be possible to arrive at a clearer definition of our categories and to determine the features truly characteristic of the Germans.

Consideration of one example—and we must be content here with a single example—will show that we can in fact obtain a clearer picture by this means. And what more convenient example can we take than that of the Germanic and Celtic peoples in the Rhineland at the beginning of the Christian era?

The distribution of particular cultural features—wheel-thrown pottery, certain types of jewellery—shows that the area east of the Rhine, extending northward to the Lippe and eastward to the Leine, looked towards the west; and this orientation is still more evident in certain associated cultural fields like religion, social structure, economic organisation and technology.

The archaeological evidence in the Rhineland throws a revealing light on the social structure of the population. An interesting feature is the existence of a number of unfortified settlements of some size alongside numerous smaller fortified sites. Some of these fortified sites may have served merely to provide temporary protection for relatively small groups of people, but others—on the evidence of their size, the length of time during which they were occupied and the nature of the material recovered—were clearly permanent fortified settlements of urban type. The most striking example of a site of this kind is the Hunnenring at Otzenhausen in the Saarland. This occupies an area of 19 hectares on a commanding hill some 600 metres high, surrounded by a massive stone wall which was reinforced by an outer wall on the more exposed side. The building of the defences involved the quarrying, transport and laying of at least 230,000 cubic metres of stone. Even these bare figures give some idea of the impressive technological and organisational achievement which these fortifications represent.

From the situation of the Hunnenring, the form of the defence works, the structure of the entrance gateways and other features we can confidently identify it as an *oppidum*, one of the fortified towns to which Caesar so frequently refers. In the course of his campaigns he had to lay siege to Alesia, Avaricum, Gergovia and Noviodunum; Alesia was captured only after the most strenuous efforts, but Gergovia successfully resisted his attack. Similar permanently occupied town sites are also found on the east bank of the Rhine, extending northwards to the edge of the upland region, as well as in Thuringia and in Bohemia and Moravia.

The population of these urban-type settlements appears to have been differentiated into various occupational groups. The implements, raw materials and manufactured articles found on the sites point to the existence of a distinct class of craftsmen; and we must assume that there were also traders living in the towns who supplied the needs of the population and found markets for the output of the craftsmen. The peasantry, however, would mostly live in villages and farmsteads in the country. The use of money, with independent coinages in the various towns, is found on both banks of the Rhine as well as in Thuringia and Bohemia.

The planning, building and administration of such large and strongly fortified settlements imply a vertically differentiated social pattern and a central authority with extensive power—that is, a structure resembling an organised state, performing the functions of a state in both war and peace. Towns of this kind were the residences and capitals of the ruling princes who are referred to by Caesar as *duces*; and it may be supposed that there were also princes of this kind in the *oppida* on the right bank of the Rhine, although none are referred to in the texts or known by name.

Summing up all the archaeological evidence on the right bank of the Rhine for the 1st century B.C., we obtain the following picture. The area to the east of the Rhine, bounded on the north by the Lippe and on the east by the upper Leine valley, belonged essentially to a culture—known as the La Tène culture from the type site in Switzerland—which at this period extended from France and Britain in the west to Bohemia, Moravia, southern Poland and Hungary in the east. It shows affinities with the central La Tène area in France and southern Germany, together with distinctive features which ally it more closely with the Moselle-Nahe area and northern France than with the heart of the La Tène culture in southern Germany and central and eastern France. These distinctive features characterise the region between the Rhine and the Leine valley as, in certain respects, a backward "fringe area" of the La Tène culture, closely connected with it but showing distinct differences in a number of significant details. The same can be said of Thuringia.

If the La Tène culture is accepted as being Celtic—and there are good grounds for this view—the region between the Rhine and the Leine must be admitted to have Celtic affinities, not in the linguistic sense but in a more general sense, with particular reference to culture.

It is only beyond the Leine and Lippe and the Thuringian Forest that we find a cultural region with a quite different pattern. We shall have more to say about this area shortly, but in the meantime the cultural phenomena in the Rhineland merit some further remarks. About the beginning of the Christian era the cultural picture in the area between the Rhine and the Leine valley changes quite suddenly. On the west bank of the Rhine Roman influence begins to make itself generally felt, gradually overlaying the indigenous culture without disturbing its essential inner continuity. The situation is very different to the east of the river. In this area many cemeteries fall suddenly out of use; urban settlements, both fortified and unfortified, are abandoned; the local coinages cease; Celtic money is no longer current, and there are at first few traces of the circulation of Roman coins. Only in the

Wetterau, the area north of Frankfurt between the Taunus and the Vogels-berg, do remains of the older culture survive.

In place of the archaeological level characterised by La Tène material we find sporadic occurrences in the early 1st century A.D. of material showing connections with the north-east. The evidence consists of small groups of burials, often with very meagre grave furnishings; large cemeteries are never found. The older burial places are avoided. The fortified sites remain empty and desolate, not to be resettled for some centuries, and no new fortifications are built. The character of the material changes in detail in the course of the 1st century—influences from the Elbe region giving place to influences from the area north of the Lippe—but the basic features remain the same for some centuries.

The ancient sources refer to a variety of population movements in the Rhine-land in the period immediately before and after the birth of Christ. Agrippa settled the Ubii on the west bank of the Rhine to protect them against attack by their enemies to the east, and the Sugambri were moved by Tiberius in an effort to pacify the region east of the Rhine. The first incomers to the region, parts of which at least were empty of population, seem to have been the Lango-bardi, coming from the north-east. They are mentioned by Ptolemy but there-after disappear from sight, giving place to the Chatti, who were to remain in occupation of the territory for centuries. Some areas which lost their popu-lation round about the beginning of the Christian era—for example the Siegerland to the north-east of Bonn—were not to be resettled for many centuries.

These developments in the region between the Rhine and the Lippe—the close cultural connections with the west in the period before the birth of Christ, the profound cultural change which took place around the beginning of the Christian era and the new links established with the north-east and later with the north—give the archaeologist an opportunity to clarify what is covered by the term Germanic and what is not. If we look at the total cultural picture revealed by archaeological evidence and consider its basic structure, we cannot regard the culture of this region in the period before the birth of Christ as Germanic. In this sense neither the Sugambri and Ubii nor the Vangiones, Nemetes and Triboci can have been Germans, even though the Romans referred to them as such. Only in the period after the birth of Christ can the culture of the region properly be called Germanic, on the evidence of its intimate connections with cultural phenomena in the Elbe-Oder-Vistula region, north-western Germany and Scandinavia. From these areas—and this is the significant point—stem the cultures of all those population groups who initiated the period of the great migrations, settled in various parts of Roman territory and are known to have spoken Germanic languages. The first of these peoples were the Alamanni, followed by the Goths and then the Gepidae, Franks and Vandals, and finally by the Bajuwari and Anglo-Saxons. We know from Icelandic literature that the Scandinavian north was also settled by such Germanic peoples.

Even though we know practically nothing of the language of the Chatti, who now settled in the Rhineland, apart from a few personal names, it is no mere unsupported hypothesis that they spoke a Germanic dialect; and the same is true of the other tribes related to them—the Cherusci, the Chauci and so on—who lived on the east bank of the Rhine.

Taking account of all the evidence, therefore, we can arrive at a coherent definition of what we mean by Germanic; and it then becomes easier to understand some of the accounts by ancient writers. It is possible, indeed, to build up from the references in ancient literature and from the archaeological evidence a picture of the relationships of the various Germanic peoples which contains no irreconcilable contradictions.

On this basis it also becomes possible to establish the boundaries of Germanic culture in the south, south-east and east. Tacitus regarded the Aestii, living on the Baltic in East Prussia, as belonging to the Germanic Suebi, although he was aware that they spoke a different language, similar to that spoken in Britain. Archaeologists now know that the Aestii cannot have been a Germanic tribe and that for a long period the Germanic settlers in East Prussia did not extend eastwards of the little coastal river Passarge. It is also known that by the beginning of the Christian era Germanic settlers had established themselves in Galicia, that about the same period Bohemia, Moravia and western Slovakia were also settled by Germanic tribes, and that as early as the time of Caesar a group of Germanic settlers had pressed eastward towards the Black Sea and occupied what is now Rumanian Moldavia and the country to the east.

It is also possible, on the basis of the archaeological evidence, to follow the development of Germanic culture and trace the areas of Germanic settlement in subsequent centuries. Some features are still obscure, like the period spent by the Goths in southern Russia, and it is not always possible to determine the particular Germanic tribe to which an object or archaeological complex belongs. In many cases, however, an exact attribution is possible. Thus we have some characteristically Germanic objects found in Italy which are clearly to be assigned to the Goths *(Plate 140)*, and we have objects from the Balkans which show close affinities with the Gothic material found in Italy *(Plate 109)*. We also have objects from southern Germany and France which must date from the time of Attila and are certainly associated with expansive thrusts by the Hunnic-Germanic-Iranian forces in Pannonia *(Plates 117–119, 121)*. The absence of Gothic material from southern France, where a Visigothic king had his capital at Tolosa (Toulouse) until about 510, is no doubt due to the situation of archaeological research in this area, for Gothic material is familiar in Spain *(Plate 141)*. Not all the Germanic material found in the Iberian peninsula, however, is Gothic: a grave containing a sword, for example, must belong to a member of some other Germanic tribe—perhaps a Vandal—for Gothic warriors were always buried without any weapons.

53

54

55

56

57

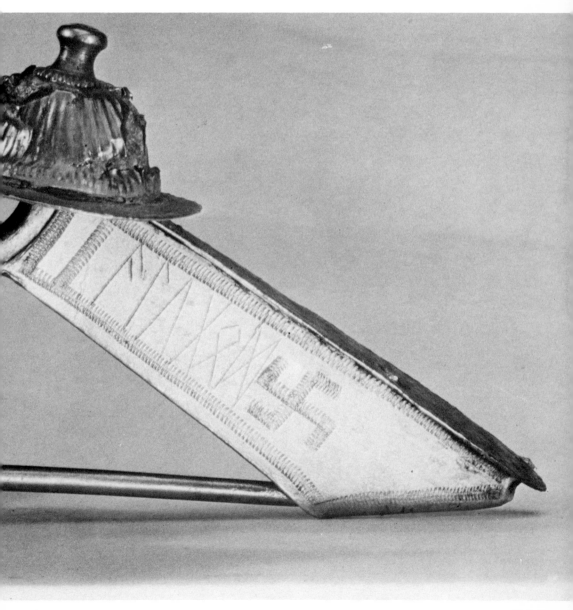

59

60

61

62

63

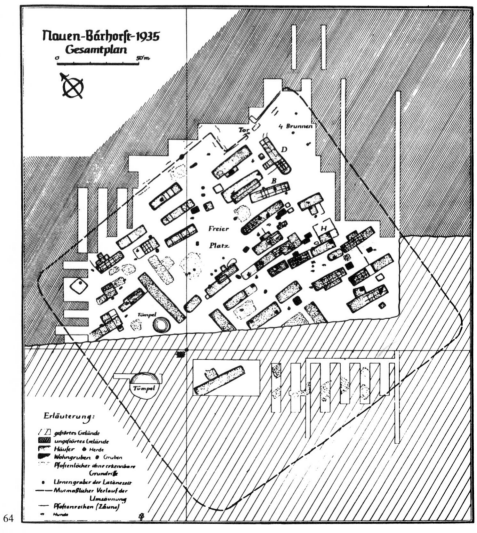

Nauen-Bärhorst-1935
Gesamtplan

0   50 m

Tor

4 Brunnen

D

B

Freier
Platz

H

Tümpel

Tümpel

Erläuterung:

gestörtes Gelände
ungestörtes Gelände
Häuser ● Herde
Wohngruben ● Gruben
Pfostenlöcher ohne erkennbare
          Grundrisse
● Urnengräber der Latènezeit
—— Mutmaßlicher Verlauf der
          Umzäunung
— Pfostenreihen (Zäune)
∽ Hunde

Just as the Goths can be identified in Italy and Spain, so the presence of the Alamanni in south-western Germany and Alsace is established by the archaeological material *(Plates 150–154, 156, 157)*. In the part of northern Gaul conquered and occupied by the Franks we have, in addition to graves belonging to Frankish warriors and noble ladies, the tomb of king Childeric (d. 482) *(Plates 125–129, 136–138, 142, 143)*. And we can even trace, however dimly and uncertainly, the course followed by the Vandals on their progress to North Africa *(Plates 146, 147)*, and by the Burgundii to Western Gaul *(Plates 148, 149)*.

Tribes and Cult Leagues

> *"At a set time all the peoples of this blood gather, in their embassies, in a wood hallowed by the auguries of their ancestors and the awe of ages. The sacrifice in public of a human victim marks the grisly opening of their savage ritual. In another way, too, reverence is paid to the grove. No one may enter it unless he is bound with a cord. By this he acknowledges his inferiority and the power of the deity."*
>
> Tacitus, Germania, 39 *(translated by H. Mattingly, Penguin Books, 1948)*.

To the archaeologist the origins of the Germanic peoples are lost in the cultures of the end of the first half of the 1st millennium B.C. About the halfway point of the millennium the archaeological evidence in northern Germany up to the borders of the upland region, in eastern Central Europe as far east as Silesia and southern Poland, and in Denmark and some Scandinavian coastal areas, reveals the existence of a number of cultural complexes—the Harpstedt group to the west, the Jastorf group in the centre and the Pomeranian culture *(Gesichtsurnenkultur)* in the east—whose contribution to the genesis of the Germanic peoples cannot be assessed in detail but in total is not open to doubt.

These Germanic tribes were peasants living mainly from stock-rearing and farming. Their fields were tilled with a simple wooden plough *(Plate 3)*. In winter the livestock—cattle, sheep and goats—lived under the same roof as the people. The horse was more important for riding than as a draught animal *(Plate 20)*. The normal pattern of settlement consisted of isolated farmsteads *(Plates 37, 38)*, groups of farmsteads *(Plates 6, 39)* or small hamlets *(Plates 8, 9)*. As the population slowly grew the hamlets developed into small villages *(Plate 64)*. Round the settlements lay the cultivated land, divided by baulks into fields of varying size *(Plate 39)*. The pattern of land use points to the existence of a right of private property in land.

Depending on economic conditions, the houses might be of substantial size *(Plates 37, 38)* or of relatively modest dimensions *(Plate 7)*. In areas where timber was available they were of solid construction with a roof of thatched straw. In the north, where wood tended to be scarce, the walls were built of turfs, with a timber framework and ridge beam supporting the roof *(Plate 9)*. These small rural communities were largely self-sufficient. A degree of economic differentiation had, however, appeared at an early period. No doubt there were specialists in various crafts—smiths, bronze-founders, carpenters —for whom farming was merely a part-time occupation. Probably, too, the manufacture of pottery was no longer a domestic activity in which each household met its own requirements, but a craft carried on in special workshops. Pottery was still, however, made by hand *(Plates 4, 5, 21, 41–45, 57, 77–81)*: the potter's wheel did not appear until the end of the 3rd or perhaps the 4th century A.D. *(Plate 76)*, and even then was not in general use everywhere.

Trade was conducted by barter: money was not used as currency, although much sought after for its metal content *(Plates 51–52, 124)*. The skills of the craftsmen showed surprising limitations in certain directions: thus although Germanic coopers were able to manufacture wooden vessels of considerable size, the art of making vessels of iron or bronze was unknown and the only metal vessels available were imported Celtic *(Plates 19, 27)* or Roman products *(Plate 52)*. The craft of shipbuilding, on the other hand, was highly developed, producing paddled boats of some size *(Plates 82, 83)* like the Hjortspring boat *(Plates 13–14)* and oar-propelled craft like the Nydam ship *(Plate 96)* which could sail the North Sea and the Baltic or make their way into the estuaries and far up the rivers.

There were no settlements of urban type in Germanic territory, and the practice of fortifying settlements, or indeed of building fortified positions of any kind, was almost unknown. Only one Germanic fortification, the Heidenschanze near Sievern, Lower Saxony *(Plate 36)*, has so far been identified: it dates from the beginning of the Christian era and cannot have remained in use for very long. The building of defensive works of this kind was inconsistent with the character of the Germanic warrior and with his method of fighting. Germanic tactics were based on a surprise onslaught by small groups of warriors, mounted or on foot: if this failed in its effect the attackers withdrew into the forest. Against superior forces like those of the Romans bogs and mosses gave better protection than any fortresses or strong points could have afforded.

The warriors' chief weapon was an iron sword. Early in the 1st century A.D. the long sword, a weapon of Celtic origin, gave place to the Roman short sword *(gladius)* *(Plates 60–63)*. In addition to his sword the warrior had one or more lances, which might be used according to circumstances for either throwing or thrusting *(Plate 59)*. There were also throwing-spears with barbs. Many warriors, however, had no sword but relied only on a lance. Frequently the lance might not even have an iron head but a pointed tip hardened by fire. The bow and arrow were known, but in the period around the birth of Christ were used only for hunting: it was not until the 4th century A.D. that they came into use again as fighting weapons *(Plates 20, 21)*. At the same period the iron throwing-axe also appeared and thereafter enjoyed great popularity.

The archaeological material from Germanic territory yields various indications of social differentiation as early as the 1st century B.C. In particular there is clear evidence of the chief's retinue of warriors as a characteristic Germanic social institution. The horsemen's tombs, richly equipped with weapons, are identified as belonging to chiefs, while the less richly provided graves are thought to belong to members of the retinue, each having a varying quantity of weapons according to his rank. (Tacitus refers to the *gradus* in Germanic society).

The development of social differentiation is seen very clearly in the 1st century A.D. in a considerable number of princely graves, richly supplied with grave goods, particularly jewellery and imported Roman vessels of bronze, silver or glass, which stand apart from the graves of ordinary people not only in the lavishness of their furnishings but in funerary ritual. Graves of this kind point to the existence of an aristocracy which not only was distinguished from the rest of the tribe but must have had connections with the aristocracy of other tribes. In this nobility we can see the forerunners of those chieftains and kings who led their forces into battle against the Roman Empire, then agreed to become *foederati*, playing their part in the defence of the Empire on the basis of a clearly defined treaty relationship, and finally set up their own dominions on Roman territory, in purely nominal dependence on the Emperor—the Ostrogoths in Italy, the Burgundii in the middle Rhône valley, the Franks in northern Gaul, the Visigoths first in southern France and then in Spain, the Vandals in Spain and later in Africa, and the Suebic Quadi in north-western Spain.

How, then, are we to define the Germans? To the archaeologist they are a population group which was distinguished by its specific culture from the Celts and their kinsmen in the west, south and south-east, and from the Balts, Slavs and Sarmatians in the east. They were a large group of peoples which had developed within a closed geographical area but had become differentiated into a number of clearly identifiable sub-groups.

The philologists have tried to establish the relationships of the various Germanic peoples on the basis of linguistic criteria and other cultural criteria which can be deduced from the linguistic evidence. Thus the East Germans seemed to be a distinct group, for they had apparently no place in the legendary division of the Germans into Ingaevones, Istaevones and Herminones of which Tacitus speaks. Since according to a tradition recorded by the 6th century historian Jordanes the Goths were supposed to have come from Scandinavia, and since there seemed to be some archaeological evidence indicating that certain other Germanic tribes had also come from the north, it was concluded that there must be a close kinship between the East Germanic tribes (Ostgermanen) and the North Germanic (Scandinavian) tribes (Nordgermanen). The other continental Germanic tribes were then labelled West Germanic (Westgermanen) in order to mark them off from the East Germanic tribes.

The archaeological evidence showed, however, that there were significant cultural differences between the Germanic tribes in the Elbe area and those in the Weser and Rhine valleys, and this led to the recognition of a separate "Elbe-Germanic" group (Elbgermanen), the term West Germanic then being confined to the tribes between the Rhine and the Weser. But since the Germanic culture of the North Sea coastal area could be distinguished from that of the West Germanic tribes it became necessary to recognise a distinct "North Sea Germanic" group (Nordseegermanèn).

It has not yet been possible to achieve a satisfactory classification of the Germanic peoples on the basis of uniform and objective criteria, although both the philological and historical sources and the archaeological evidence hold out some possibilities in this direction. Admittedly any such attempt would come up against certain inherent difficulties, since the internal structure of the Germanic peoples must have changed profoundly and sometimes very rapidly over the centuries. Nevertheless for certain periods—e.g. the period round about the beginning of the Christian era—the sources are relatively abundant and reliable, and it seems possible to sketch out a picture of the subdivisions of the Germanic peoples which contains no essential inconsistencies.

Post-Caesarean ethnographic theories offered two different classifications of the Germanic peoples. The one given by Pliny, although the earliest we have, is not presented in its original form but has been altered and extended—no doubt by Pliny himself—to fit in with the circumstances of his time and the information then available. Tacitus's classification, although later in date, certainly represents the original tradition. The great 19th century scholar Karl Müllenhoff recognised that Tacitus's classification was not complete, excluding as it did the East Germanic peoples. It seems likely, however, that the area to which it applied was even more restricted, although it is a matter of great difficulty to define it exactly. The three groups mentioned by Tacitus—the Ingaevones, Istaevones and Herminones, whom we may conveniently refer to collectively as the Mannus tribes, after the name of their legendary ancestor—are also mentioned by Pliny and other authors. Pliny gives little information about the tribes belonging to these groups, Tacitus none at all. According to Tacitus the Ingaevones lived nearest the sea; and Pliny tells us that the Chauci belonged to this group. The Cimbri and Teutoni, who are also mentioned by Pliny, were evidently inserted at a later date for some particular purpose. Tacitus notes that the Herminones lived "in the middle"; and Pliny includes in this group not only the Chatti and Cherusci but also the Suebi and Hermunduri. He also says that the Istaevones lived close to the Rhine. (The text we have mentions the Cimbri as well, but this is clearly an error).

Tacitus adds that the Marsi, Gambrivii, Suebi and Vandilii were ancient tribes not included in the tripartite classification. His Vandilii are clearly to be identified with Pliny's first group, the Vandili; and there is general agreement that this group falls outside the main tripartite division of the Mannus tribes. Although it is not generally accepted that the Suebi should also be excluded, it seems necessary to follow Tacitus in this too. Pliny grouped them and the Hermunduri with the Chatti and Cherusci, which is certainly wrong on two counts. In the first place the Hermunduri were a section of the Suebi, who would thus be included twice; and moreover none of the other sources suggest that there was any particularly close connection between the Cherusci and the Suebi.

Thus it is clear that the Mannus tribes represented only a small part of the population of Germanic stock—a group which occupied the area to the west of the Suebi, taking in the Weser and Rhine valleys and extending up to the North Sea. The tripartite division of the Mannus tribes is evidently of legendary and religious significance. The list of the tribes given by Pliny is certainly not complete; but the only other tribes which can be shown to have belonged to the group are the Batavi and Canninefates, who according to Tacitus were originally part of the Chatti.

It would clearly be wrong to assign all the tribes living in the western part of Germanic territory to the group of Mannus tribes. There is some evidence to suggest that the main area of settlement of this group originally lay fairly far to the east—perhaps beyond the Ems; and this leaves open the possibility that many tribes which originally lived farther west belonged to other groups. The feature which in the case of the Mannus tribes is only dimly perceptible, being suggested allusively by the mythological origin of the tribes, is clearly recognisable in the case of the Suebi: they were a cult league, a religious association of tribes. Tacitus tells us of their holy place, "shared by all the peoples of this blood", where the all-powerful deity dwelt, and to which at set times came embassies from all the Suebic tribes—the Langobardi, Hermunduri, Marcomanni, Quadi and Semnones—to make their sacrificial offerings.

A third cult league, in addition to the Mannus tribes and the Suebi, consisted of the tribes of the Cimbrian peninsula and the Danish islands which owed allegiance to the goddess Nerthus and had a central shrine dedicated to her on one of the islands—Funen or more probably Zealand. Tacitus also tells us that the Marsi in the Rhineland had within their territory the "temple" of the goddess Tanfana, "the most revered holy place of these peoples"; and no doubt this shrine was also frequented by other unnamed tribes belonging to the same cult league as the Marsi. Presumably the Marsi were the chief tribe in their cult league, as the Semnones were the chief tribe in that of the Suebi.

The holy place of the Naharvali was probably the cult centre for a number of eastern tribes, in particular the Lugii. It is not clear, however, what was the relationship of Pliny's Vandili (Tacitus's Vandilii) to the Lugii. According to Pliny the Burgundii, Varini, Charini and Goths belonged to the Vandili, while Tacitus assigns the Helvecones, Manimi, Helisii, Naharvali and Harii to the Lugii. Since the Harii correspond to the Charini there was clearly a connection between the two groups. It looks as if the Lugii, Goths and Burgundii (who are not mentioned by Tacitus), together with a number of smaller tribes, made up the cult league of the Vandilii.

The changes in the structure of the Germanic peoples during the early centuries of our era were so far-reaching that from the time of the great migrations onwards we find entirely new names—Franks, Alamanni, Bajuwari—cropping up alongside older names like the Burgundii, the Vandals, the Suebi and the Goths. And even these older names now represent new or much altered structures.

Notwithstanding the discrepancy between the archaeological and the literary sources and their differing evidential value, they do come into clear and direct concordance in the case of the cult leagues. The archaeological evidence for the period around the birth of Christ allows us to identify areas with differing burial types and gives us some impression of Germanic religious conceptions —or, more precisely, burial practices. From the point of view of the funerary

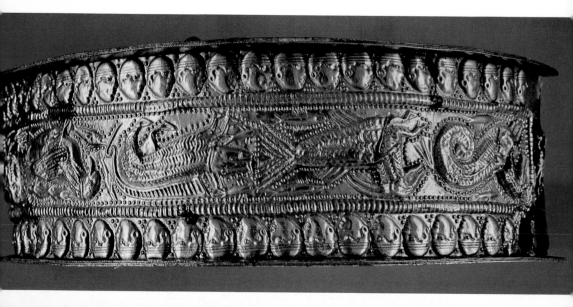

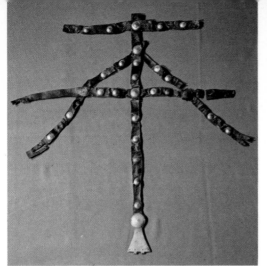

77

78

79

80

81

82, 83

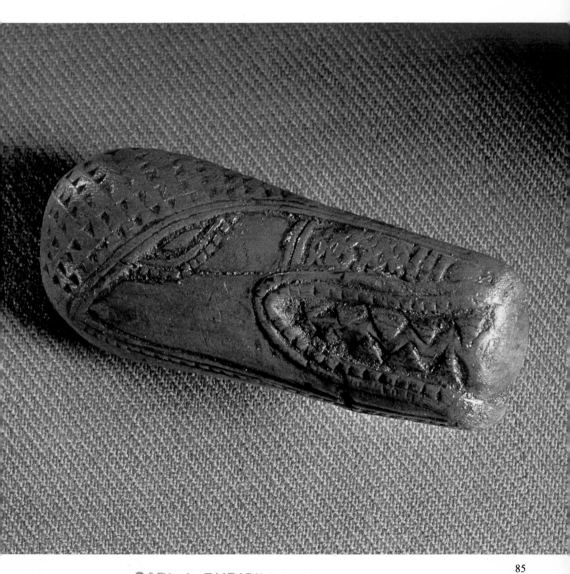

85

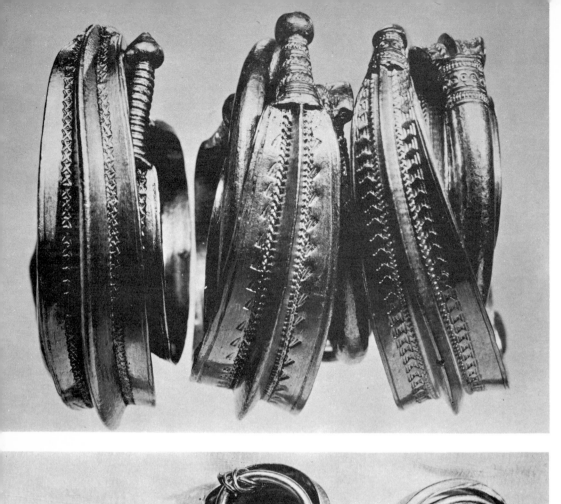
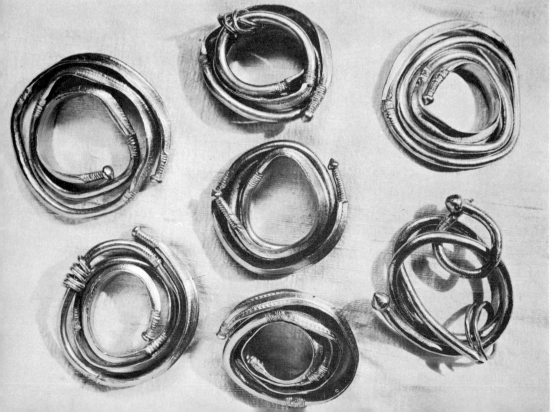

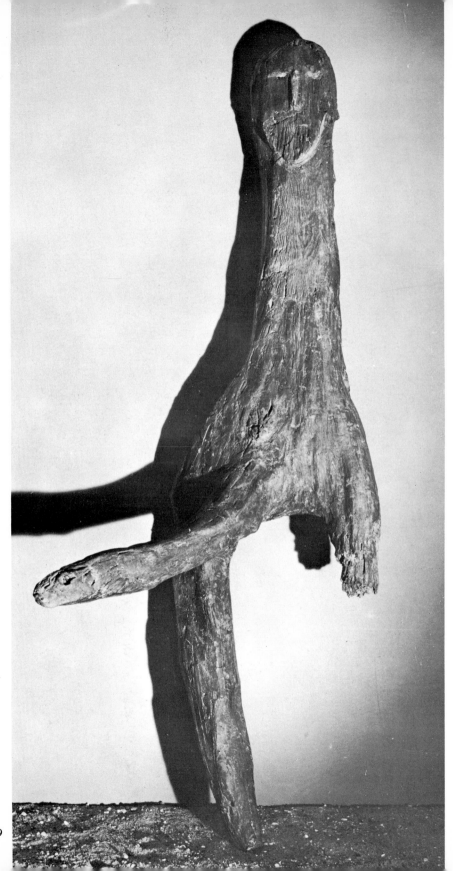

cult these areas reflect the existence of cult leagues with identical or very similar practices. On the basis of the archaeological data we can distinguish the following areas (*Grabritenkreise*) with characteristic burial practices: the "Elbe-Germanic" culture *(Plates 24–26, 41, 49, 57, 64)*, extending from the lower Elbe area in the north, by way of the Altmark, Brandenburg, Thuringia and Saxony, to Bohemia, Moravia and western Slovakia in the south; the "West Germanic" culture in the area between the Rhine and Weser and on the North Sea, and later also in Thuringia *(Plates 22–23, 42–45, 51–52)*; and the Oder-Vistula group in Silesia, central and southern Poland and Masovia *(Plates 60–63, 71, 73, 76)*. These three areas clearly correspond to the cult leagues of the Suebi, the Mannus tribes and the Vandilii. In other cases the relationships between cult groups which can be identified from the written sources and the areas with distinctive burial practices as revealed by archaeology are still not clear.

These relationships are unlikely in any event ever to be fully clarified, largely because the written evidence is too meagre but also because Germanic culture, like any other culture, was never static but subject always to a process of change. This can be clearly demonstrated by archaeology, but it was less evident to the ancient authors. They observed and recorded mainly a series of events which took place on the Roman frontiers, with some indication of the background to those events. They were often dependent on authorities of dubious value and tended unwittingly to juxtapose information relating to different periods. This makes it difficult to achieve a reconciliation of all the available evidence.

The accounts of the ancient authors suggest that the Germanic tribes were of much greater importance as politically active groups than the cult leagues. Tacitus devotes a whole chapter of his *Germania* to the tribal structure of the Germanic peoples but makes only the briefest of references to cult leagues. The archaeological evidence, on the other hand, throws much more light on the cult leagues, the tribal structure being discernible only in the background.

Clearly there is a certain "subjectivity" in the sources. The ancient observers were conscious in the first place of the dynamic elements in Germanic society—those particular groups which played an active rôle in history. Tacitus's interest in Germanic customs is an exceptional case. The archaeological evidence, however, tends to reveal the "static" aspects of Germanic culture, the general and less rapidly changing factors which influenced the action of particular groups.

The archaeological material thus reveals more clearly than the ancient written sources the important part which religion played in the life of the Germanic peoples. The most significant feature of their social structure, along with the family and the kinship group, was undoubtedly the cult league—although the individual man and woman at the time may have been less conscious of this than the present-day archaeologist. We are struck by the general cultural concordances within the cult leagues, extending far beyond the religious field. Much of the secular material associated with a particular cult league shows specific features found throughout its whole area. This may be to some extent due to the fact that cult leagues were at the same time economic associations through which, by contacts between one settlement and another, particular products became generally known and imitated, so that they took on similar forms throughout the area. But there is also another, deeper, reason: many objects of everyday use had a religious significance in addition to their primary social or economic function.

A few examples will illustrate this. The "funnel urn" (*Trichterurne*) of the Elbe-Germanic culture *(Plate 26)*, as we know from examples found on settlement sites, was used for ordinary domestic purposes, but it also had a specific cult function as a container for cremation burials, being used for this purpose only in the burial of males. The lance was the Germanic warrior's favourite weapon: it was not merely a weapon, however, but frequently bore luck symbols and runes *(Plate 59)* which gave it magical force. A richly decorated fibula was no doubt primarily an ornament worn by a woman on special occasions *(Plate 58)*, but it too might be inscribed with signs and runes giving it a magical function. A drinking-horn was used at feasts and carouses, but it undoubtedly also had a part to play in cult ceremonies, in which we know that the drinking of beer was an important element. Drinking-horns ending in ox-heads emphasise the cult function of the horns, and the figured ornament and number symbolism of the two gold horns from Gallehus *(Plates 97–98)* indicate that these horns were intended for cult purposes.

In order to serve its purpose every object had to possess some magical virtue. This is evident where an article bears a runic inscription *(Plates 53, 58, 97–98, 100)*, for the magical function is made explicit in the inscription. But this magical virtue did not flow only from runes but was conveyed by a variety of other luck symbols which might be inscribed on the object *(Plates 33–34, 60, 81, 97–98, 104–106)*. A belt might bear magical signs *(Plates 33–34)*; or a fibula in the form of a boar *(Plate 51)* might endow its wearer with the strength of the god Frey, whose attendant animal was a boar.

Thus the world of the Germanic peoples was charged with magical forces, and almost every object and every human activity had its religious aspect.

GERMANIC RELIGION

III

The Gods

> *"They do not, however, deem it consistent with the divine majesty to imprison their gods within walls or represent them with anything like human features. Their holy places are the woods and groves, and they call by the name of god that hidden presence which is seen only by the eye of reverence."*

Tacitus, Germania, 9.

(Quotations from Tacitus in this section are in the translation by H. Mattingly, Penguin Books, 1948).

We are separated from Germanic religion by more than the centuries which have passed since the disappearance of an independent Germanic culture. Our capacity to comprehend it is limited not only by the lapse of time and the restricted and one-sided sources of information at our disposal. These are not the only difficulties which make it a hazardous undertaking to treat phenomena widely separated from one another in time and place as forming part of a unified system. The question must also be asked whether there was in fact any such unified system at all, or merely a number of different systems with certain identical or similar features. The greatest difficulty, however, is that of understanding the concepts we are dealing with: how can we hope to comprehend the religious beliefs of a people so remote from us, separated by so many centuries during which very different religious categories have come to be taken for granted and accepted as natural? One thing at any rate is certain: Germanic religion was quite different from other religions familiar to us, and neither Christianity nor Greek mythology offers a satisfactory approach to its comprehension.

But there are still other difficulties to be faced. One such difficulty is that the northern part of Germanic territory is so outstandingly rich in religious

109

documents during the later period—that is, some centuries after the Christian faith had been accepted farther to the south—and the southern area so remarkably poor in a much earlier period. Frequently this may merely mean that the north preserved into later centuries religious practices which had also existed in the south at an earlier period: indeed the north may well have taken over particular features of its religious beliefs from the south. The scattered pieces of evidence from the south, where Germanic religion was displaced by Christianity at a relatively early stage, can often be fitted into their proper place in the more amply documented mythology of the north; and the material from the north often serves to support, supplement or confirm the limited information we can glean from the south. We cannot, however, uncritically accept the northern material as valid for the whole of Germanic territory. The north undoubtedly contributed distinctive elements of its own—and this not only because it had a longer period of development in which to do so. It may also have lost many features which existed in the south. The northern world was different from the south, with its own ways and its own needs. And there is the further complication that most of our evidence from the north is in literary form—that is, it is religion transmuted into art—and that the works concerned were composed, or at any rate written down and given their final form, after the introduction of Christianity. Snorri's world was already imbued with Christian feeling, and Christianity had brought many Greek and Roman concepts with it to the north. It is true, of course, that in early times religious beliefs and literary expression were closely related, and that the thinking and aspirations of primitive communities were always shot through with religious conceptions; but nevertheless the two spheres were distinct and by no means to be identified with one another. Not everything in the literature of early periods is an expression of religious belief, and not all religions are exactly as they are represented in literature.

In the light of these and other considerations we soon realise how inadequate is the available evidence on the religious beliefs and practices of the continental Germanic peoples—at any rate if we are looking in the first place to the written sources. The archaeological material, on the other hand, is abundant in both the north and the south, although somewhat limited in scope, being concerned mainly with the cult of the dead. The evidence about the worship of the gods is very scanty; and even what we have is often vague and difficult to interpret. It is not always possible to reconcile the written sources with the evidence yielded by archaeology: thus Tacitus's statement that the Germans had no images of their gods is contradicted by the archaeological evidence. We have figures of both gods and goddesses *(Plates 16–17, 53, 89–95)* dating from quite early periods—well before the time of Tacitus. There are also many animal figures *(Plate 56)* which were probably cult images. The ox-head on a fibula *(Plate 31)* and the animal's head at the end of a drinking-horn no doubt also had a religious function. As a rule, however, it is not possible to identify the divinity who is represented or alluded to.

Thor, known in the south as Donar, is an exception to this rule. The Nordic myths describe him as a tall handsome figure with a full red beard, a keen eye which none could withstand and a loud voice, which was amplified still further by his beard. The beard was a distinctive feature which set him apart from other gods and makes it easy to identify his cult images. In the later period, when the influence of Christianity had begun to make itself felt, there were many temples dedicated to his cult. In the earlier period certain places were regarded as sacred to him, and at such places an image of the god would be set up, roughly hewn from a conveniently shaped piece of timber. A wooden figure with a beard, represented with the attribute of his generative power *(Plate 89)*, was found in a cairn in a bog at Broddenbjerg in Jutland. Elsewhere the god was represented in dual form, as a symbol of fertility and as a post bearing a bearded head *(Plates 90–91)*. In another cairn found in a bog at Rosbjerggård in Jutland a fragment of another cult image was recovered, nothing being left but the stumps of legs.

Of the manner in which these images were worshipped, however, the archaeological material gives no direct information. Accounts in northern literature refer to worship by invocations and libations. The act of libation involved dedicating a brimming cup to the god and drinking it off in a gesture of adoration; and in fact fragments of numerous vessels were found at the feet of the Broddenbjerg and Rosbjerggård figures—the very cups which had been drained in honour of the god and then smashed to pieces.

Among the female divinities, it is perhaps possible to identify the goddess Nerthus who is mentioned by Tacitus. His account indicates that she was worshipped in the area west of the Baltic as Mother Earth—that is, the goddess of fertility. She took an interest in human affairs and travelled about among the various peoples. "In an island of Ocean stands a sacred grove, and in the grove stands a car draped with a cloth which none but the priest may touch. The priest can feel the presence of the goddess in this holy of holies, and attends her, in deepest reverence, as her car is drawn by kine. Then follow days of rejoicing and merry-making in every place that she honours with her advent and stay. No one goes to war, no one takes up arms." Is it pure chance that two ceremonial wagons *(Plates 10–11)* of very similar type, of carved wood with applied metal ornament, were found in a bog at Dejbjerg in Jutland? On one of the wagons, which has survived almost complete, is a seat—perhaps intended for the goddess, who would be thought of as invisible. A number of highly stylised female bronze figures found in Denmark, with marked emphasis on the abdomen and breasts, are evidently fertility symbols, and it is tempting to see them as representations of Nerthus. After the goddess's progress among men the wagon was restored to its "temple"; and Tacitus adds: "After that the car, the cloth and, believe it if you will, the goddess herself are washed clean in a secluded lake. This service is performed by slaves who are immediately afterwards drowned in the lake." The slaves were thus offered as a human sacrifice to the goddess.

The existence of similar practices in other parts of Germanic territory is attested by the Byzantine writer Sozomen, who tells us that in the year 348

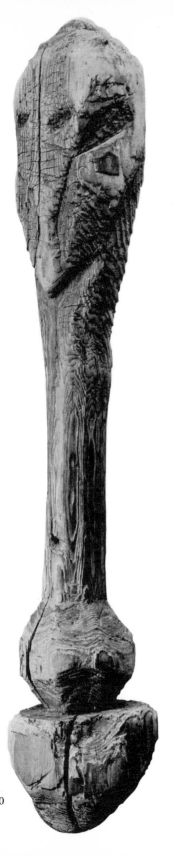

90

91

92

93

94

95

97

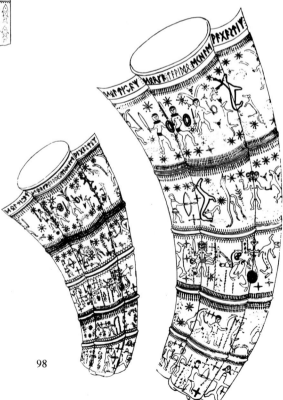

98

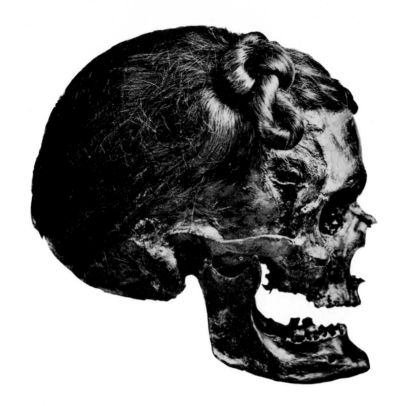

99

100

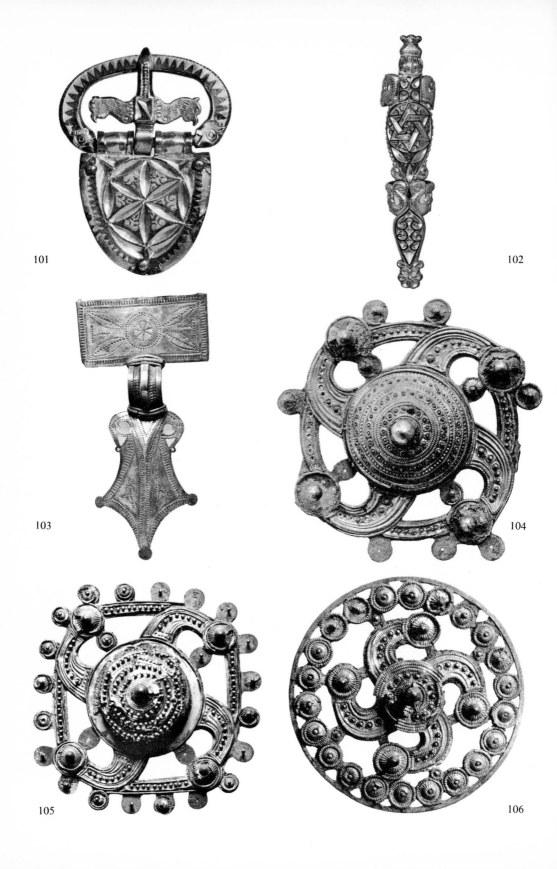

101

102

103

104

105

106

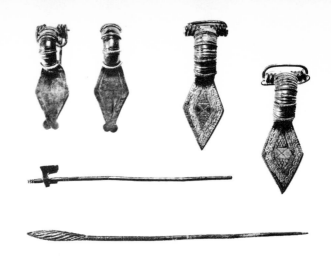

108

109

110

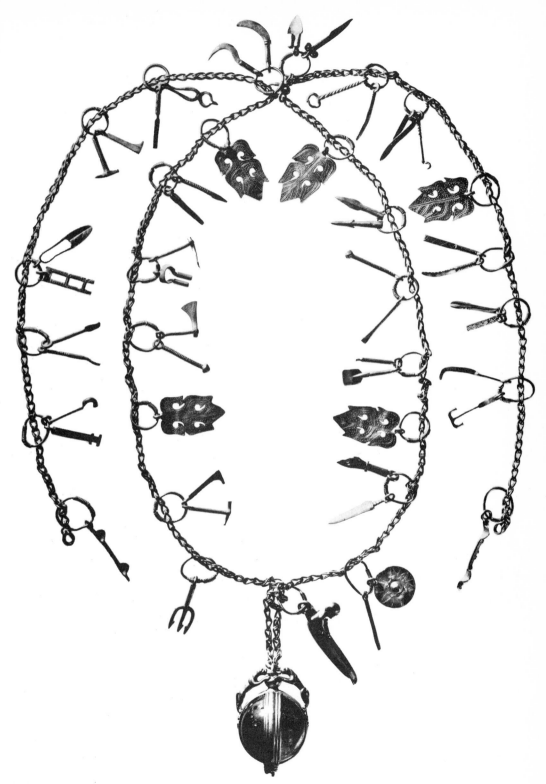

112

113

114

115

116 →

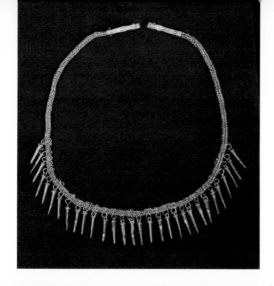

117

118

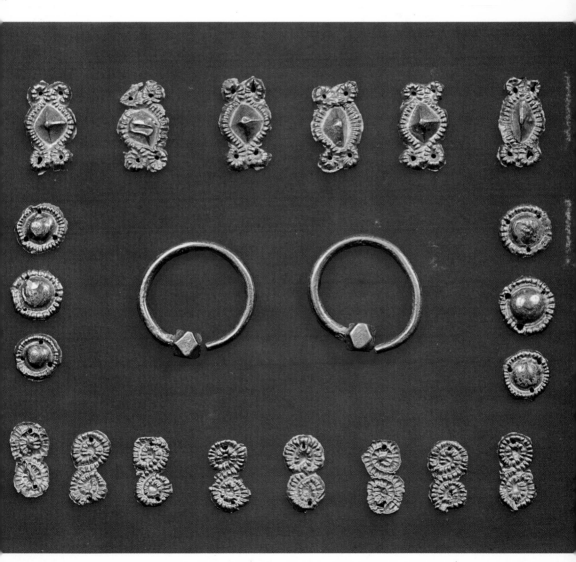

119

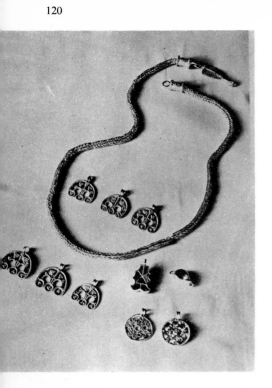

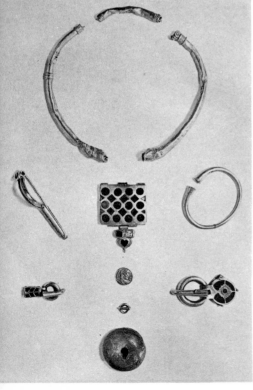

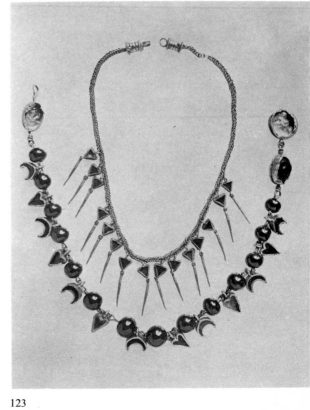

125

126

127

128

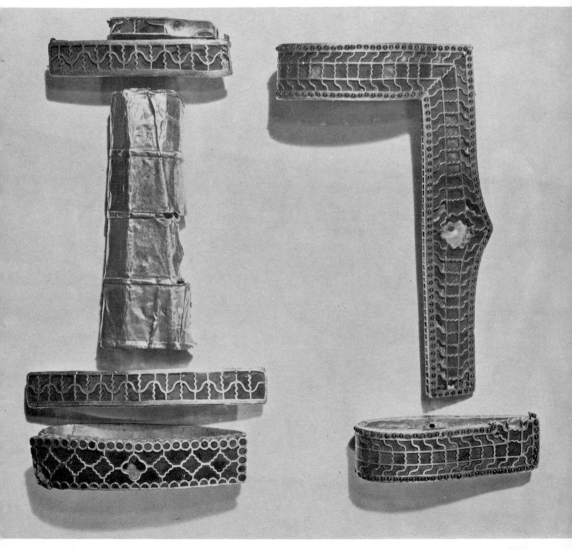

129

the Visigothic king Athanaric caused a statue to be carried in procession through the settlements of the Christianised Goths, requiring all men to worship it and make offerings to it; any who refused to comply were put to death. Sozomen evidently misinterpreted the meaning of this pagan ritual, seeing the killing of the Christians as the main purpose of the procession and not as the purely incidental circumstance that it was.

The reference to Nerthus's sacred lake is a reminder that lakes, bogs and mosses played an important rôle in Germanic religion. Here offerings were made to the divinities and perhaps also to beings who inhabited the legendary realm intermediate between gods and men. Evidence of the practice comes mainly from the great bog finds in north-western Germany and the regions along the west of the Baltic. Among the most striking examples are the large hoard of rings found at Smederup in Jutland *(Plate 2)*, dating well back into pre-Christian times; the boat and weapons found at Hjortspring on the island of Als *(Plates 12–14)*, dating from the 1st century B.C.; the oared ships *(Plate 96)*, weapons, implements and ornaments found at Nydam; and the great find at Thorsberg in the district of Angeln, which yielded the richest and finest jewellery we possess *(Plates 65–69)*.

Tacitus asserts that the Germans had no temples, but himself contradicts this statement by his reference to the temple in which the cult wagon of the goddess Nerthus was housed after her annual progress among men, and his reference in another passage to the temple of the goddess Tanfana. So far, however, we have no archaeological evidence to indicate what these temples were like.

A site at Borremose in Jutland *(Plate 9)*, occupied in the 1st century A.D. by a small village settlement, consisted in its earlier phase of a walled enclosure with a structure in one corner which may possibly have been a temple. This site has, however, less resemblance to the temples of a later period in Scandinavia and Iceland, which show the influence of Christian churches, than to the Celtic cult sites known as *Viereckschanzen*. Since the Borremose site is the only known example of its kind on continental Germanic territory, and since there were strong southern Celtic influences in the region west of the Baltic at the time it was in use, we cannot exclude the possibility that it represents merely an isolated reflection of Celtic cult practices which had no wider influence in other parts of Germanic territory.

The marking out of the cult precinct with wattle fences—evidently very similar to those used in the early building phases of the Celtic *Viereckschanzen*—is attested on a number of sites in Germanic territory. Two typical examples are the votive sites of Thorsberg *(Plates 65–70)* in the district of Angeln and Vimose *(Plate 85)*, the sacred bog on the island of Funen. The evidence yielded by the excavation of the votive site of Oberdorla in Thuringia is of particular interest. At various points on this site there had been posts with cult images surrounded by circular wattle-fenced enclosures up to 20 metres in diameter. In these enclosures the remains of animal and human sacrifices were found; and it was clear from the nature of the animal bones recovered that they were not merely ordinary food residues. The bones consisted almost exclusively of skulls and shank bones, mostly from cattle, much more rarely from pigs, sheep, goats or horses. In contrast the food residues found on the contemporary settlement site in the vicinity consisted predominantly of pig bones.

The Germanic divinities were—inevitably—thought of in the likeness of men. They had the same characteristics as human beings, enlarged to a god-like scale. They could suffer in the same way as ordinary men and women and, like mankind, they knew deceit and treachery. In the legendary tale recounting the origin of the Langobardi, for example, Wodan's wife Frea deceived him for the benevolent purpose of enabling them to achieve victory over the Vandals.

Gods and men, indeed, were related by kinship, since the leading families were descended from gods. Thus there seems to have been a traditional story among the Ostrogoths that the Amali were descended from the Aesir; and Snorri records in the *Heimskringla* that the Ynglings who ruled in Uppsala traced their origin to Odin. Similarly in the Anglo-Saxon genealogies all the leading families are shown as descending from Wodan. Wodan was the god who granted victory; and what could be more appropriate for the old noble families, the leaders of the community and ancestors of the later chieftains of warrior bands, than a line of descent going back to the god of war himself?

A pagan god must as a matter of course have a weapon as his attribute. In northern mythology Odin's weapon was a spear—an arm also borne by Wodan—while Thor had his hammer. The old storm god and conductor of the dead had no enemy to encounter against whom he would need to use a sword in hand-to-hand fighting: his proper weapon was a spear, which could be hurled through the air to strike from a distance. Snorri tells us in the *Heimskringla* that when Odin was on his deathbed he caused himself to be marked with the point of his spear, so that all who died in arms should be his liege men.

The *Edda*, however, tells a story, putting these words in Odin's mouth: "I know that I hung nine nights long on the windy tree, wounded by the spear dedicated to Odin—myself given to myself!" He had been hung in the tree by giants who were his enemies, and had neither food nor drink; then, in his extremity, he saw below him some runes. "Down I bent, took up the runes, took them up moaning: then down I fell." The runic spell had released him from his noose, and he had in the same moment discovered for himself the magical power of runes. Thereafter he became the master of runic lore; and his spear Gungnir—which legend said was made, like all weapons, by dwarfs—bore runic signs which reinforced its magical power.

Of Wodan—the southern counterpart of Odin who was, perhaps, derived from him—no similar story is told; but since the runes were undoubtedly developed in southern Germanic territory and runic spells on lance-heads form a strikingly high proportion of the oldest runic inscriptions, the conclusion is inescapable that Odin's association with runes comes from the south and is derived from Wodan. We also find Wodan as a master of magical lore in the second Merseburg charm:

> *Phol ende Uuodan vuorun zi holza.*
> *du uuart demo Balderes volon sin vuoz birenkit.*
> *thu biguol en Sinthgunt, Sunna era suister;*
> *thu biguol Friia, Volla era suister;*
> *the biguol en Uuodan, so he uuola conda:*
> *"sose benrenki, sose bluotrenki,*
> *sose lidirenki:*
> *ben zu bena, bluot zi bluoda,*
> *lid zi geliden, sose gelimida sin!"*

> Phol and Wodan went to the wood.
> Then Balder's foal wrenched a foot.
> Then chanted Sinthgunt and Sunna her sister,
> Then chanted Friia and Volla her sister,
> Then chanted Wodan, as he well knew how:
> "As the bone-wrenching,
> As the blood-wrenching,
> As the limb-wrenching:
> Bone to bone, blood to blood,
> Limb to limb, be they joined again!"

As a god of war Wodan was entitled to receive sacrifices; and accordingly the victorious Cherusci sacrificed their Roman prisoners to him. The Hermunduri sacrificed the Chatti whom they defeated in 59 A.D. Of the Goths we are told that "they had ever honoured Wodan with a grisly cult, offering him the lives of their prisoners captured in war, in the belief that he who determined the outcome of battles must of necessity be appeased by human blood. To him were the first fruits of victory promised, in his honour were captured arms and armour hung in trees. They felt a peculiar and inherent reverence for him, since they thus believed themselves to be paying divine honours to him who was the forefather of their race" (Jordanes).

Only rarely does archaeology yield evidence of such human sacrifices. In the Late Bronze Age ramparts at Lossow, near Frankfurt on the Oder, numerous shafts up to 7.50 metres deep, filled with animal bones and broken human bones, were found above the latest occupation level, which dated from the middle of the 1st millennium B.C. Although these sacrificial pits cannot be precisely dated, the connection with Germanic rites of human sacrifice seems very plausible. The god, however, was entitled not only to human victims but to a share of the booty won in war; the material found at Hjortspring, therefore, may well have been an offering to Wodan *(Plates 12–14)*.

Offerings were made to other gods as well as to Wodan, and the votive gifts comprised not only prisoners or booty captured in war but also jewellery, as in the Brodelbrunnen ("Bubbling Well") at Bad Pyrmont *(Plates 51–52)*, or pottery, like the thirty vessels found close together in the Lundtoft bog along with many sheep's bones, or agricultural produce like animals or animal fat.

The offerings were made in the place where the god dwelt; and he might dwell not only in particular places but in particular objects. It seems probable that the figured representations which become increasingly common in the 3rd century A.D. depict divinities, the representation of a god being conceived as containing the divine power within a material object. The gods could, however, emerge whenever they pleased from the place or object within they dwelt and become visible to their friends, either in a dream or in the full light of day. Thus the world of the gods and the world of men might meet at any time. Between man and god there was a difference not of kind but of degree. The boundary between gods and men was always there, but its position might be varied according to circumstances, being lower down when a man was engaged in his daily round, higher up when he was making an offering to the gods or setting out for war. Ordinary men possessed less of the divine force than chiefs; and the king possessed it in such abundant measure that it was often vain, on that account alone, to oppose him.

The Cult of the Dead

> "*A quite incalculable amount of twisted gold was loaded upon a wagon; and the old king was carried up to Hronesness. The people of the Geats prepared for Beowulf, as he had asked of them, a splendid pyre hung about with helmets, shields, and shining corselets. Then, mourning, the soldiers laid their loved and illustrious prince in the midst. Upon the hill the men-at-arms lit a gigantic funeral pyre. Black wood-smoke whirled over the conflagration; the roar of flames mixed with the noise of weeping, until the furious draught subsided and the white-hot body crumbled to pieces. Sadly they complained of their grief and of the death of the king.*"
>
> Beowulf, 3134–9.
>
> (*Quotations from Beowulf in this section are in the translation by David Wright, Penguin Books, 1957*).

We possess an abundance of evidence on the Germanic cult of the dead, for—even apart from the main votive sites and the material found there—the most important and most numerous finds of Germanic material come from graves, where both the objects themselves and the context in which they are found are primarily and essentially of religious significance.

The scene described in the account of Beowulf's funeral must have been enacted on countless occasions: the dead man would be laid on his bier, his widow would wail her lament, the other mourners would add their voices to the chorus—the "*carmina diabolica*" as they were known to Christians, to whom everything pagan was of the Devil. The body would be placed on the funeral pyre together with the grave goods—the man's garments and weapons, the woman's clothing, jewellery and domestic equipment, and all the various objects belonging to the departed which they would need to have with them for their life in another world. Then the pyre would be lit and allowed to burn down, after which the tomb would be built (in the case of Beowulf a burial mound with various internal structures in timber), the charred remains of bones collected from the ashes and the dead man's possessions would be deposited in the tomb, and it would then be closed up. And then would come the final scene as it is described in *Beowulf*: "Then twelve chieftains, all sons of princes, rode round the barrow lamenting their loss, speaking of their king, reciting an elegy, and acclaiming the hero. They praised his manhood and extolled his heroic deeds."

Not every funeral was as lavish and elaborate as Beowulf's, even allowing for a measure of poetic licence in the account that has come down to us. Cremation, however, was evidently the form of burial originally practised throughout Germanic territory, although perhaps in varying forms. The cremated remains might be buried in a simple pit or in a pottery vessel *(Plates 22–23)*. The grave goods were deposited in the pit or in and around the urn. A mound was raised over the grave, or sometimes there might be practically nothing to be seen on the surface—perhaps no more than a few stones or a post to mark the spot. Towards the end of the 1st century B.C.—that is, some considerable time before the arrival of Christianity—inhumation *(Plate 50)* came into use alongside cremation. Being the accepted Christian method of burial, inhumation in due course displaced cremation; but in the peripheral parts of Germanic territory cremation long continued in use.

In *Beowulf*, which was given its final form in England, the idea of cremating the dead may have survived as a reminiscence of older practices. The poem describes the funeral of the Danish warrior Hnaef, who was killed in Friesland, on a pyre similar to that of Beowulf himself.

At the time when the action of *Beowulf* took place, in the 5th century A.D., the practice of inhumation was already general in the southern part of Germanic territory. Thus the Visigothic king Alaric I, dying in southern Italy, was not cremated but buried by inhumation. The same is true of the Visigothic king Theodoric, killed in the battle of the Catalaunian Fields against the Huns in 451. His praises were sung in the lamentations of his followers: "Tears were shed, but only such as customarily flow in mourning for a brave warrior. For it was a glorious death, as the Huns themselves bore witness, so that even the enemy's pride appeared to be humbled when they were thus compelled to stand idly by while such a great king was buried with all his honours about him. But the Goths performed all the funeral rites for Theodoric as duty required and bore off their illustrious leader amid the clash of weapons" (Jordanes). The burial took place on the battlefield on which the king had fallen.

Even Attila himself, king of the Huns, whose power was based on the allegiance not only of the Huns themselves but of various dignitaries of predominantly Germanic and probably also of Iranian and Sarmatian origin, seems to have been buried with ceremonies similar to Germanic rituals. The Byzantine historian Priscus of Panicn tells us: "His mortal remains were laid on a bier under silken canopies in the midst of a field. Then the Huns carried out a splendid ceremony. The best horsemen of the whole Hunnish people rode round the place where he lay, as in the games of the circus, glorifying his great deeds in funeral dirges, after the following fashion: 'Attila, the exalted one, commander of the Huns, son of Mundzuk, ruler of warlike peoples, he who ruled alone with mighty power over the kingdoms of Scythia and Germany as none other before him had done, the terror of the two Roman empires, the conqueror of cities! Rather than expose all else to plunder, he

131

132   133

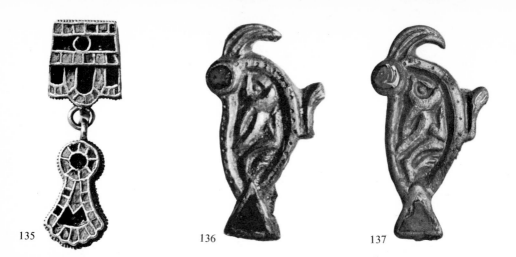

135   136   137

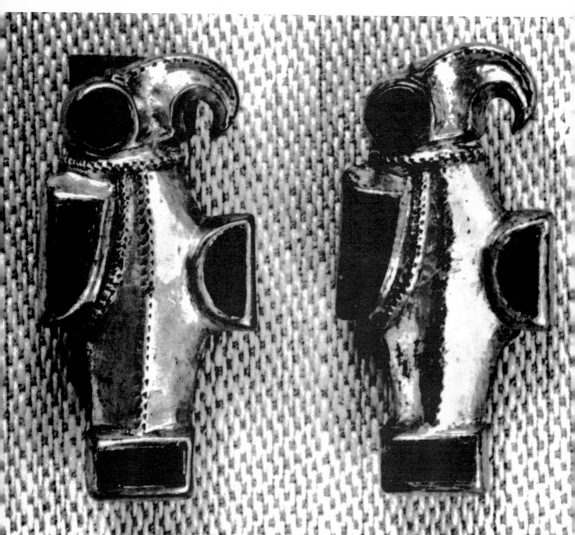

138

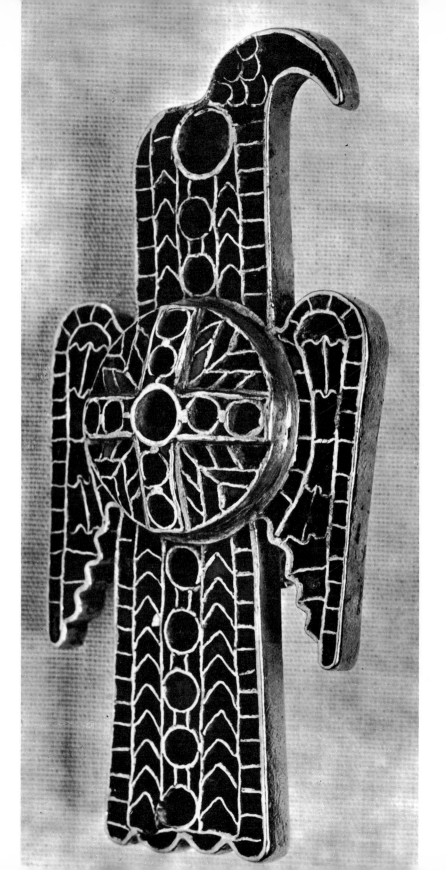

139

140

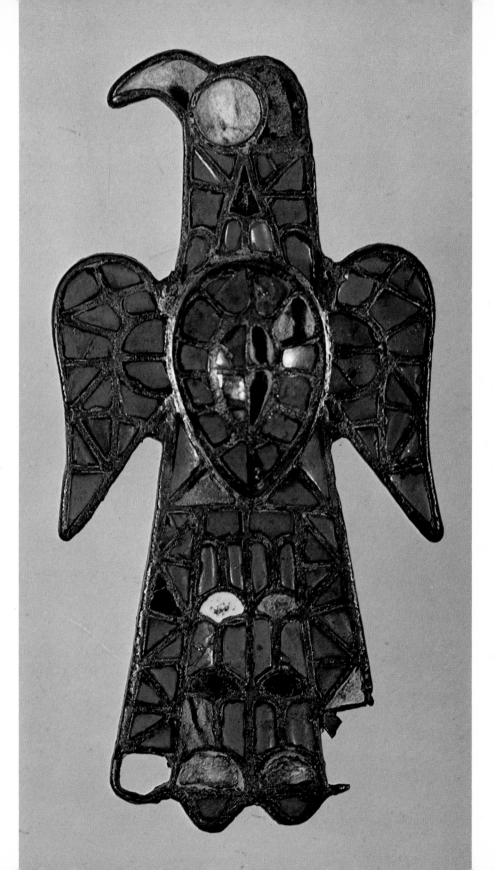

141

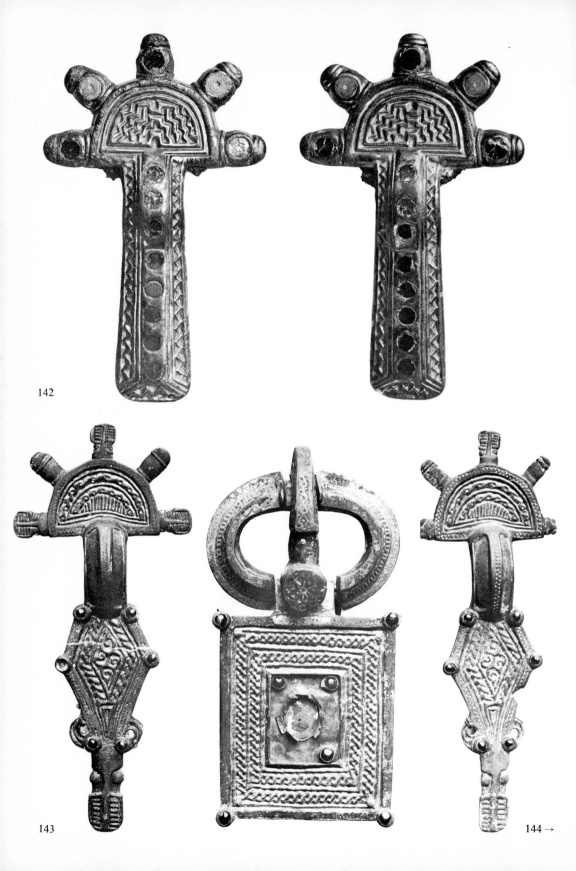

142

143   144 →

146

147

149

150

151

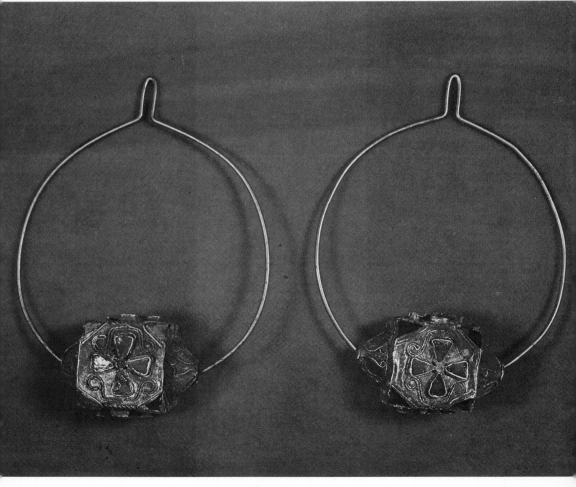

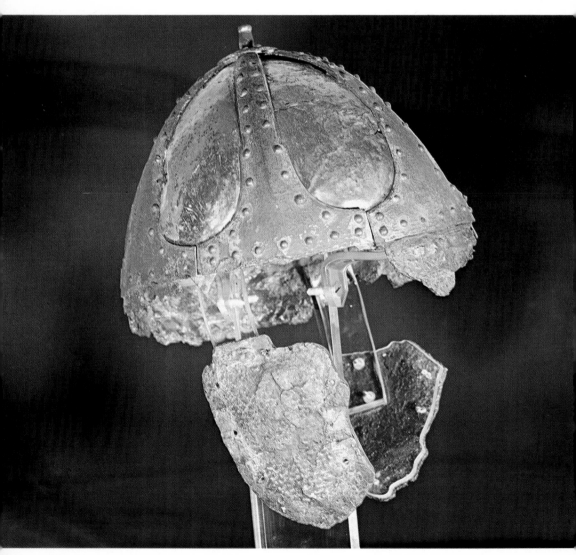

deigned to accept an annual tribute. After his splendid achievements he met his death not through a wound inflicted by the enemy, not through any treachery by his own followers, but from grief—and that in the full joy of success, in his people's hour of glory. Who then shall consider this the end of life, when no man thinks of vengeance?' After mourning him with such lamentations they held the ceremony they call a *strava* on his burial mound. with a most riotous carousal. Thus the extremes were brought together, and the funeral lament was interspersed with effusions of joy. Then in the stillness of night they committed the body to the earth. His first sarcophagus was made of gold, the second of silver, the third of iron." Here we have a detailed account of the funeral lament, perhaps not verbally accurate but at any rate reproduced by Priscus in broad outline on the basis of the reports he had been given of the ceremony.

Here again we find mention made of the valuable offerings which accompanied the dead man. The weapons he had won from defeated enemies, rich horse trappings and a variety of other marks of distinction were laid in the grave along with him; and "in order that the curiosity of men should be kept at a distance from such great riches" (Jordanes) those who carried out the work were put to death. This was also done after the burial of Alaric. The reason given for the killings, however, was certainly not the true one. Who could have disturbed Alaric's grave, lying as it did under the waters of the Busento? And who could have failed to see Attila's tomb, a tall burial mound set in the wide Pannonian plain? In both cases the killing of the slaves for the reason stated would have been quite pointless. The real purpose must have been to offer a human sacrifice in honour of the mighty dead.

The graves of Alaric, Theodoric and Attila have not been found and probably never will be. Chance, however, has revealed a fair number of princely graves—some belonging to people unknown to history, others to men and women whose names are recorded and sometimes famous. At Leg Piekarski in Poland several graves belonging to noblemen of the early 2nd century

A.D. were discovered, containing silver drinking cups and various bronze vessels. One particularly well known burial is the richly furnished tomb of the Frankish king Childeric, father of Clovis, who died in 482 A.D. and was buried at what is now Tournai in Belgium *(Plates 125–129)*, where the Frankish kings then held their court. The tomb, found as long ago as 1693, contained a large quantity of valuable objects, some of which have since disappeared—e.g. a double-edged long sword with a gold-mounted hilt and scabbard, both set with red semi-precious stones (almandines), a single-edged short sword, also ornamented with gold and almandines, an iron throwing-axe, a gold bracelet and much else besides.

Even more famous is the tomb of the Ostrogothic king Theodoric in Ravenna, built for him by a Syrian architect about 520 A.D. It is totally different from any other ancient Germanic funerary monument known to us, consisting as it does of a two-storey main structure with a ten-sided base containing the cruciform burial vault, an upper storey of smaller diameter and a flattened dome made from a single slab of Istrian limestone. It is a building of impressive severity of form, with no obvious prototype in ancient architecture unless perhaps the Mausoleum of Hadrian (Castel di S. Angelo) in Rome. It might be thought of as a Germanic burial mound transposed into architectural form, except that no Ostrogothic burial mounds are known. The architectural conception, however, is Germanic, for the object was "to build a vaulted structure in which the body of the dead man could be preserved without being deposited in the ground, so that the living were no longer required to squander their substance on the dead or to see the body of one they loved cast without honour into the grave."

In this monumental tomb Theodoric was buried in 526. It must have been richly furnished with grave goods in accordance with the practice of the Goths. But he was not destined to lie there long: barely twenty-five years later his body was torn rudely out of the sarcophagus as that of a heretic, along with all the grave goods. A gold helmet facing which was found near the tomb in 1854 but was stolen from the Ravenna Museum in 1924 may have been among them.

It is clear from the objects deposited in graves that the Germanic peoples believed in a very real life after death—although, of course, the selection of objects was not primarily determined by the nature of the afterlife but by the actual possessions of the dead man or woman. The dead warrior was entitled to retain his weapons, a woman needed all her clothing and jewellery, and in all cases food and drink must be available.

As we have noted, the dead were either cremated or inhumed, cremation being the original form, practised almost exclusively in the earlier period, and inhumation a later development. The real significance of cremation to the Germanic peoples, however, is difficult to establish, and it is correspondingly difficult to understand the reason for the change from cremation to inhumation. The suggestion that inhumation was a practice taken over from some southern people does not get to the essence of the matter and is not even literally accurate.

Men continued to exist after death, but in a different fashion. The vital force was thought to be contained in the breath, and was therefore located in the head; and it was believed that when a man died this vital force withdrew into his head but could thereafter re-emerge. But how the life of the dead man was conceived cannot be deduced from the archaeological material and can be only faintly discerned in the written sources.

The conception of the afterlife as a place of delight, a kind of earthly paradise, is never found in southern Germanic territory in the pre-Christian period. The dead man was thought of as spending his time in or near his tomb, and he might sometimes—although this was evidently exceptional—be a source of disturbance to the living. In the Icelandic saga of Grettir the Strong we are told of Kar the Old that "since Kar died the place has been so

haunted that he has driven away all the farmers who had steadings here."
Whereupon, the story goes on, Grettir sets off for the burial mound, descends
into it, makes a hole in the timber wall of the tomb chamber and forces his
way in; then, after a fierce struggle with the dead man, he succeeds in cutting
off Kar's head and fixes it between his thighs, so preventing the severed parts
of the body from joining up again and putting a stop to Kar's troublesome
activities.

The dead man was thought of as existing in an intermediate realm of the
living dead which was quite close to the world of the living. He remained in
the element familiar to him in life and was still a warrior, a peasant or a
seafarer as he had been before. This conception finds its perfect expression
in the story of Helgi in the *Edda*. A maid says to Sigrun, wife of the dead
Helgi: "Go out, Sigrun of Seva Fell, if your wish be to find the leader of
the people! Home has come Helgi, the howe is open. The spear-wound
bleeds: the king asks that you dry the drops." And so Sigrun goes to Helgi
in his burial mound and says: "Now am I glad to find you, like Odin's fal-
cons, greedy for sustenance, when they smell a battle or some warm prey,
or, damp with dew, gaze on the red of dawn. Now will I kiss you, dead king,
ere you put off your bloody coat of mail. With hoar-frost, Helgi, your hair
is white; dripping your breast with the dew of battle; clammy the hands of
Hogni's son-in-law. How shall I, lord, heal your sorrow?" And Helgi replies:
"Excellent drink have we still to drink, though life and land be lost! Let
none sing dirges for us, though our breasts be pierced by spears! Now is the
maid, the lord's daughter, come to bear me company here in the howe."
But at the first light of morning Helgi must rise and ride away: he must be
with Odin's army of the dead "before the cock in the hall rouses the victorious warriors". In the evening the maid watches on the grave mound,
and then Sigrun herself comes again: "Wished he to come, Sigmund's
son would have come from Odin's hall ere now. Hope of Helgi's home-
coming now burns low." And indeed Helgi never returns, and Sigrun,
grief-stricken, does not long survive him.

Thus the dead man was not really dead, and accordingly he could come to life again in the person of a kinsman. The practice of naming a newborn baby after one of the famous dead is well attested in both the northern and southern parts of Germanic territory. In the Icelandic *Svarfdaela Saga* Thorolf, wounded to death, says to his brother Thorstein: "For myself I wish only one thing—that if a son is granted to you he should be named Thorolf. All the good fortune that is in me shall I give to him: then may I hope that my name shall remain alive so long as the world is inhabited by men."

The practice of naming an infant after a dead man, so that he should live on in the child and transmit his good fortune to him, is found among the Visigoths and also among the Franks. Thus Pepin the Short was named after his dead grandfather Pepin of Heristal; and Charlemagne was given the name of his grandfather, Charles Martel, who had died six months before his birth. In this respect ancient pagan ideas long survived under cover of Christianity.

The conception of the survival of the dead in an intermediate world closer to this life than the life beyond is clearly a reflection of ancient Germanic beliefs; and the idea lingered on into the Middle Ages. Thus in the mediaeval chronicle of Ekkehard of Aura it is recorded that during the First Crusade, in 1096, Charlemagne appeared and took part in the fighting; and in the year 1197 the monk Gottfried of Cologne reports that "Theodoric, who of old ruled in Verona", had appeared in human form and supernatural size, riding a black horse, and had warned of the dangers looming over the realm.

Into this intermediate world the dead could ascend; but so too could the gods descend into it. A Swedish chronicler records—expressly asserting the correctness of his information—that in the year 1208, four days before a decisive battle between the Danes and the Swedes, Odin appeared to a blacksmith in southern Norway asking to have his horse shod. Almost at the same time Snorri tells us that, according to the Swedes, Odin had been in the habit of appearing to them before great battles were fought.

In the later period there is some evidence pointing to a belief that only when a man's body was completely destroyed was he really dead—that is, finally annihilated. The practice of cremation then acquires a particular significance quite distinct from the original conception. That a dead man who was malicious and troublesome could be expelled from the intermediate realm by the burning of his body is made clear in the story of Hrapp in the *Laxdaela Saga*.

Hrapp was a ruffianly character who was first buried, at his own request, under the threshold of his kitchen. "In that way," he said, "I shall be able to keep a closer watch on the running of the house." But when he began to go about the district causing all kinds of harm he was dug up and reburied under a heap of stones at a remote and lonely place. Then, when he continued making a nuisance of himself, he was dug up again; and since his body was still undecayed a pyre was erected, Hrapp was burned on the pyre and his ashes cast into the sea. Thereafter, we are told, no one was disturbed again by his haunting. Thus only consumption by fire was believed to kill the dead man once and for all; but for greater security his ashes were scattered over the sea, so that he should no longer have any place where he could permanently dwell.

It seems to us incredible that the Athanasians should have torn the body of Theodoric—a Christian like themselves, but an Arian—out of his sarcophagus a quarter of a century after his death, burned his bones and dispersed the remains. But this was the beginning of a process of turning the great Gothic king into a creature of the Devil which reached its height in the monkish writings of the Middle Ages—the counterpart of the Germanic ele-

166

vation of the dead Theodoric into the intermediate realm close to the world of the living, as found in Scandinavia.

In later times the practice of burning as a form of capital punishment extended over the whole area subject to Germanic law. Boniface tells us that it was the custom among the Saxons to compel fallen women and adulteresses to hang themselves and then to burn their bodies. Burning was also thought an appropriate penalty for incendiarism. It was, moreover, seen as a convenient means of preventing sorcerers and witches from returning to trouble the living.

These practices may well reflect the survival of very ancient Germanic ideas, modified in specific directions. They presuppose that the normal burial practice was inhumation, but may also perhaps represent a continuation of the old custom of cremation, which differed from inhumation in not locating the vital force of a dead man in the corpse's head.

In the mythology of the Nordic countries, transmuted though it may be by literary art, 'he change from cremation to inhumation can be observed; but evidently the authors of the sagas were no longer fully conscious of the religious significance of the practices they recorded. "After his death Odin was burned, and the burning took place with great ceremony. In those days it was believed that the higher the smoke rose into the air the higher the dead man was raised in heaven, and the more of his possessions he took with him the richer he would be." Here Snorri gives an interpretation, already incorporating Christian elements, which he had found in the older writings he used as his source. The Germanic peoples, of course, did not believe in a heaven in the Christian sense. Nevertheless there may be a reminiscence in this passage of more ancient conceptions. The Arab traveller Ibn Fadhlan, who was present at the cremation of a 10th century Viking chief on the Volga, mentions as a notable circumstance the strong wind which rose while the pyre was blazing. In *Beowulf* we are told of the fierce flames which "swirled to the clouds" at Hnaef's funeral, the assumption being that the dead man was drawn up into the clouds along with the flames and smoke.

We are inevitably reminded of Tacitus's reference to the army of the Harii in the *Germania*. This eastern Germanic tribe, he tells us, used trickery and careful timing to secure an advantage over their enemies: "They black their shields and dye their bodies black and choose pitch dark nights for their battles. The terrifying shadow of such a fiendish army inspires a mortal panic, for no enemy can stand so strange and devilish a sight." These practices of the Harii reflect a belief in an army of the dead which travelled through the air; and the counterfeit of this army summoned up all the terror associated with the original conception.

Thus the dead were not thought of as being tied to their burial place and its surroundings. This suggests a connection with the Einherjar of the Nordic sagas, the chosen band of warriors whom Odin gathered round him after their death. Is the conception of the Einherjar a late one, or are we merely dealing here with a late literary expression of a very ancient idea in which the dead man was freed from his body by the process of burning? Certainly Odin was a late arrival in the Scandinavian north, and in Iceland he was of little importance compared with the countrymen's god Thor; only in the sagas did he achieve his preeminent position.

Among the continental Germanic peoples Wodan, the counterpart to the Nordic Odin, was one of the principal gods at a quite early period; but here too he seems to have attained special importance at a relatively late stage. There is a good deal of evidence to suggest that he displaced the older sky god Tiu and took over some of his functions.

On this basis the army of the dead which travelled through the clouds would originally be Tiu's retinue of warriors. Then, if we are correctly interpreting what Tacitus says, the *regnator omnium deus* worshipped in the sacred grove of the Semnones was the sky god Tiu. It should be noted that the cremation of the dead was then still generally practised among the Suebi.

It is tempting to pursue our deductions still farther. Can we, for example, detect any relationship between Wodan's rise to importance and the beginnings of inhumation among the Germanic peoples? It is quite certain, however, that the origins of the practice are to be sought in a variety of different directions. Among the Vandili, for example, the first use of inhumation is attested before the beginning of the Christian era; and there seems to be no connection between these burials and the rich noblemen's tombs of the Elbe-Oder-Vistula area in the 1st and 2nd centuries A.D. Even the boldest speculations fail to carry conviction; and for the present, therefore, the origins of the practice of inhumation must remain an open question.

CONCLUSION

Among the numerous specialised fields of archaeology that of the Germanic peoples occupies a place by itself. This can perhaps be more easily illustrated by specific examples than by theoretical and methodological discussions, and accordingly can probably best be appreciated at the conclusion of this study.

The first factor to be noted is the present situation of archaeological research in Germanic territory. There is perhaps no part of the world, with the exception of the Holy Land, which has been the object of such thorough archaeological study as central and northern Europe. Scandinavian, Dutch, German, Polish, Czech and Austrian archaeologists have been carrying on intensive research and exploration in their various countries for something like a century now, with valuable assistance from a host of interested amateurs and non-professionals. In consequence of all this activity the amount of material available to the specialist has become almost unmanageably large.

A correspondingly large effort has been devoted to the study of the material recovered. The literature on the archaeology of the Germanic peoples already amounts to a library of several thousand volumes, and original contributions of outstanding importance have been made by such great scholars as the Swede Oskar Montelius and the Norwegian Ingvald Undset, the German Gustaf Kossinna and his Polish disciple Josef Kostrzewski.

In the study of Germanic culture the literary sources are of particular importance in supplementing the archaeological material. In Mesopotamia, of course, there is the cuneiform literature, in Egypt we have a large body of hieroglyphic documents, and the volume of surviving Greek literature is not inconsiderable. The written sources on Germanic culture are notable not so much for their abundance as for their heterogeneity: Greek and Roman scholars have left us accounts of the ethnography of the Germans, late authors like Cassiodorus and Isidore of Seville wrote the history of some of the Germanic peoples, Ulfilas translated the Bible into Gothic. After the unity of the Germanic peoples had been lost in the great migrations the individual peoples developed literatures of their own, sometimes still written in Latin and sometimes in the Germanic vernaculars, which produced historical works, religious writings and poetry of high literary quality. This literature reflects the circumstances of an earlier period and must be studied by anyone seeking to achieve a comprehensive picture of Germanic culture and history. Nor can archaeology afford to neglect or ignore these extensive literary sources.

The abundance of the sources yields an almost inexhaustible supply of information about the Germanic peoples; and yet there are many gaps in our knowledge. The heterogeneity of the sources, moreover, increases the methodological difficulties which face the archaeologist in every field of study but are less visible and as a result less troublesome the more homogeneous his sources are. Germanic archaeology therefore exemplifies a variety of problems of archaeological method.

Another distinctive feature of Germanic archaeology is that the culture with which it is concerned was not not a highly developed one like the Greco-Roman, Mesopotamian, Iranian, Egyptian and other cultures of the ancient world. The archaeological material which it recovers is, therefore, of quite a different character. In other areas archaeologists are of course using the same groups of material—burials, hoards of valuable objects, settlement sites—to obtain information about the particular culture with which they are concerned; but the proportions of the various groups vary considerably from place to place. Where in Germanic territory are palaces to be found like those of Assyria or Babylon? Or a temple like the Temple of Amon at Karnak? Where in the Germanic world is there any art to compare with the art of Greece? All these things, and many others besides, are lacking; for Germanic culture represented a beginning, not a perfected achievement. But, on the other side of the account, where else have we such an abundance of evidence on the cult of the dead? In what other cultures do we know so much about the forms of agricultural economy? Where else have we such a wealth of detail on social groupings, tribal divisions and the native aristocracy? Where else have we such a range of information about pottery types, jewellery, implements and weapons? Or about the patterns of trade?

Thus we have an abundance of material, yielding not only much detailed factual information but also some perception of connections and relationships. All of this, however, relates to the different aspects of a life which is quite remote from us. Given this abundance of material, and the variety of problems which it raises for the archaeologist, it has been possible in this study to consider only three particular aspects: the meaning of the term Germanic, the territory occupied by the Germanic peoples in the period around the birth of Christ, and Germanic religious conceptions. None of these problems has been completely solved, and none of the solutions discussed in this book is universally accepted. This is, of course, the mark of a field of study which is in process of continuing advance.

The picture of Germanic culture which we have sought to draw is—deliberately—incomplete. The crafts of the Germanic peoples, their technology, their economic history have been merely touched on in passing. Problems of social structure and social history have been barely mentioned. The development of Germanic art has not been discussed.

The reader may be surprised, indeed, that so little space has been devoted to Germanic art, to whose distinctive character so many examples cited in this study bear witness. Surely the artists of the Germanic peoples, he may ask, deserve some discussion? The answer must be that Germanic art, more readily perhaps than some other aspects of Germanic culture, can be left to speak for itself.

CHRONOLOGICAL TABLE

	NORTHERN EUROPE			CENTRAL EUROPE	
1000					1000
900	Viking period			Mediaeval period	900
800	———	808: Haithabu (Hedeby)		———	800
700	Vendel period				700
				Merovingians	
600	———				600
500	Migration period	482: † Childeric		———	500
		426: † Theodoric		Migration period	
400	———			———	400
300	*2nd Period* From Severus to Arcadius	260: Limes		*2nd period* From Severus to Arcadius	300
200	———		Roman Empire	———	200
100	*1st period* Caesar, Flavians, Antonines	9: Haltern 8: Battle in Teutoburg forest (Varus)		*1st period* Caesar, Flavians, Antonines	100
B.C.					B.C.
	Seedorf period	52: Alesia		D	
100	———	102: Aquae Sextiae		———	100
200	Jastorf period		La Tène period	C	200
300	———			B	300
400	——— ?			A	400

(center spanning label: Roman Empire — between Northern and Central Europe columns)

175

BIBLIOGRAPHY

General Works

N. ÅBERG, *The Anglo-Saxons in England during the Early Centuries after the Invasion*, Uppsala, 1926.

N. ÅBERG, *Die Franken und die Westgoten in der Völkerwanderungszeit*, Uppsala, 1922.

H. ARNTZ and H. ZEISS, *Die einheimischen Runendenkmäler des Festlandes*, Leipzig, 1939.

J. BRØNDSTED, *Danmarks Oldtid*, III, 2nd ed., Copenhagen, 1960.

J. BRØNDSTED, *The Vikings*, Penguin Books, 1960.

C. COURTOIS, *Les Vandales et l'Afrique*, Paris, 1955.

R. HACHMANN, *Goten und Skandinavien*, Berlin, 1970.

R. HACHMANN, G. KOSSACK and H. KUHN, *Völker zwischen Germanen und Kelten. Schriftquellen, Bodenfunde und Namengut zur Geschichte des nördlichen Westdeutschlands um Christi Geburt*, Neumünster, 1962.

R. H. HODGKIN, *A History of the Anglo-Saxons*, I–II, 3rd ed., London, 1952.

W. KRAUSE, *Die Runeninschriften im älteren Futhark*, Göttingen, 1966.

P. NØRLUND, *Wikingersiedlungen in Grönland. Ihre Entstehung und ihr Schicksal*, Leipzig, 1937.

H. REINERTH (ed.), *Vorgeschichte der deutschen Stämme*, I–III, Berlin, 1940.

L. SCHMIDT, *Geschichte der deutschen Stämme bis zum Ausgang der Völkerwanderungszeit*, I, *Die Ostgermanen*, 2nd ed., Munich, 1934.

L. SCHMIDT, *Geschichte der deutschen Stämme bis zum Ausgang der Völkerwanderungszeit*, II, 1, *Die Westgermanen*, Munich, 1938.

J. WERNER, *Beiträge zur Archäologie des Attila-Reiches*, Munich, 1956.

J. WERNER, *Münzdatierte austrasische Grabfunde*, Berlin and Leipzig, 1935.

D. WILSON, *The Anglo-Saxons*, London, 1960.

Regional Studies

E. ALBRECTSEN, *Fynske jernaldersgrave*, I, *Førromers jernalder*, II, *Ældre romersk jernalder*, III, *Yngre romersk jernalder*, Copenhagen, 1954, 1956 and 1968.

O. ALMGREN and B. NERMAN, *Die ältere Eisenzeit Gotlands*, I–II, Stockholm, 1914 and 1923.

W. D. ASMUS, *Tonwarengruppen und Stammesgrenzen in Mecklenburg während der ersten beiden Jahrhunderte nach der Zeitwende*, Neumünster, 1935.

C. J. BECKER, *Førromersk Jernalder i Syd- og Midtjylland*, Copenhagen, 1961.

E. BENINGER and H. FREISING, *Die germanischen Bodenfunde in Mähren*, Reichenberg (Liberec), 1933.

E. BENINGER, *Die Germanenzeit in Niederösterreich von Marbod bis zu den Babenbergern*, Vienna, 1934.

E. BENINGER, *Die germanischen Funde der späten Kaiserzeit und des frühen Mittelalters in Mittelfranken*, Berlin, 1962.

H. J. EGGERS, "Grabfunde der Völkerwanderungszeit aus Pommern", *Baltische Studien*, new series, 46, 1959, 13–27.

J. ERDNISZ, *Die Chauken. Ihre räumliche Abgrenzung auf Grund der Bodenfunde*, Würzburg, 1939.

A. GENRICH, *Formenkreise und Stammesgruppen in Schleswig-Holstein nach geschlossenen Funden des 3. bis 6. Jahrhunderts*, Neumünster, 1954.

R. GUTHJAHR, *Die Semnonen im Havelland zur frühen Kaiserzeit*, Greifswald, 1934.

W. HEYM, "Der ältere Abschnitt der Völkerwanderungszeit auf dem rechten Ufer der unteren Weichsel", *Mannus*, 31, 1939, 3–28.

J. IONIȚĂ, "Contribuții cu privire la Cultura Sîntana de Mureş-Cerneahov pe Teritoriul Republicii Socialiste România", *Arch. Moldovei*, 4, 1966, 189–259.

E. KIVIKOSKI, *Die Eisenzeit Finnlands*, I–II, Helsinki, 1947 and 1951.

O. KLINDT-JENSEN, *Bornholm i Folkevandringstiden og Forudsætningerne i tidlig Jernalder*, Copenhagen, 1957.

J. KMIECINSKI, *Zagadnienie tzw. Kultury Gocko-Gepidzkiej na Pomorzu Wschodnim w Okresie Wczesnorzymskim*, Lodz, 1962.

G. KÖRNER, *Die südelbischen Langobarden zur Völkerwanderungszeit*, Hannover, 1938.

J. KOSTRZEWSKI, *Die ostgermanische Kultur der Spätlatènezeit*, I-II, Würzburg, 1919.

F. KUCHENBUCH, "Die altmärkisch-osthannoverschen Schalenurnenfelder der spätrömischen Zeit", *Jahresschrift für Vorgeschichte der sächsisch-thüringischen Länder*, 27, 1938, 1–143.

R. LASER, *Die Brandgräber der spätrömischen Kaiserzeit im nördlichen Mitteldeutschland*, I, Berlin, 1965.

M. B. MACKEPRANG, *Kulturbeziehungen im Nordischen Raum des 3.–5. Jahrhunderts*, Leipzig, 1943.

W. MATTHES, *Die nördlichen Elbgermanen in spätrömischer Zeit*, Leipzig, 1931.

G. MILDENBERGER, *Die germanischen Funde der Völkerwanderungszeit in Sachsen*, Leipzig, 1959.

C. A. MOBERG, *Zonengliederungen der vorchristlichen Eisenzeit in Nordeuropa*, Lund, 1941.

K. MOTYKOVA-ŚNEIDROVA, *Die Anfänge der römischen Kaiserzeit in Böhmen*, Prague, 1963.

K. MOTYKOVA-ŚNEIDROVA, *Weiterentwicklung und Ausklang der älteren Kaiserzeit in Böhmen*, Prague, 1967.

A. von MÜLLER, *Formenkreise der älteren römischen Kaiserzeit im Raume zwischen Havelseenplatte und Ostsee*, Berlin, 1957

A. von MÜLLER, "Völkerwanderungszeitliche Körpergräber und spätgermanische Siedlungsräume in der Mark Brandenburg", *Berliner Jahrbuch für Vor- und Frühgeschichte*, 2, 1962, 105–189.

B. NERMAN, *Gravfynden på Gotland under tiden 550–800 e. Kr.*, Stockholm, 1919.

B. NERMAN, *Die Völkerwanderungszeit Gotlands*, Stockholm, 1935.

W. NOWOTHNIG, *Brandgräber der Völkerwanderungszeit im südlichen Niedersachsen*, Neumünster, 1964.

E. NYLÉN, *Die jüngere vorrömische Eisenzeit Gotlands*, Uppsala, 1956.

COUNT E. C. G. OXENSTIERNA, *Die Urheimat der Goten*, Leipzig, 1945.

COUNT E. C. G. OXENSTIERNA, *Die ältere Eisenzeit in Östergötland*, Linköping, 1958.

R. M. PERNIČKA, "Geographische Ausbreitung und Charakter der Besiedlung Mährens in der römischen Kaiserzeit", *Sbornik Prací Fil. Fak. Brnenské Univ.*, 13, 1964, 53–65.

C. PESCHECK, *Die frühwandalische Kultur in Mittelschlesien*, Leipzig, 1939.

A. PLETTKE, *Ursprung der Angeln und Sachsen*, Hildesheim and Leipzig, 1921.

H. PREIDEL, *Die germanischen Funde in Böhmen und ihre Träger*, I–II, Kassel, 1930.

R. ROEREN, "Zur Archäologie und Geschichte Südwestdeutschlands im 3. bis 5. Jahrhundert n.Chr.", *Jahrbuch des Römisch-Germanischen Zentralmuseums*, 7, 1960, 214–294.

B. A. RYBAKOV (ed.), "Chernyakhovskaya Kultura" ("The Chernyakhov Culture"), *Materialy i Issledovaniya po Arkh. SSSR*, 82, 1960.

V. SAKAR, "Mladší dolsa rímská v podkrušnohorské oblasti" ("The later Roman Empire in the Erzgebirge"), *Pamatky Archeologické*, 57, 1966, 604–648.

U. SALO, "Die frührömische Zeit in Finnland", *Finska Fornminnesföreningens Tidskrift*, 67, 1968, 9–249.

R. SCHINDLER, *Die Besiedlungsgeschichte der Goten und Gepiden auf Grund der Tongefäße*, Leipzig, 1940.

W. SCHLEIERMACHER, "Die Burgunden am Limes", *Varia Archaeologica*, Berlin, 1964, 192–194.

B. SCHMIDT, *Die späte Völkerwanderungszeit in Mitteldeutschland*, Halle, 1961.

M. STENBERGER, *Öland under äldre järnålder*, Stockholm, 1933.

M. STRÖMBERG, *Untersuchungen zur älteren Eisenzeit in Schonen*, I–II, Lund, 1961.

B. SVOBODA, *Čechy v dobe stehovány národu* ("Bohemia in the Period of the Migrations"), Prague, 1965.

E. A. SIMONOVICH, "Pamyatniki chernyakhovskoy kultury stepnogo poddneproviya" ("Remains of the Chernyakhov Culture in the Dnieper Steppe Region"), *Sovetskaya Arkh.*, 24, 1955, 282–316.

K. TACKENBERG, *Die Wandalen in Niederschlesien*, Berlin, 1925.

F. TISCHLER, "Der Stand der Sachsenforschung, archäologisch gesehen", *35. Bericht der Römisch-Germanischen Kommission, 1954*, 1956, 21–215.

R. v. USLAR, *Westgermanische Bodenfunde des 2. bis 3. Jahrhunderts n.Chr. aus Mittel- und Westdeutschland*, Berlin and Leipzig, 1938.

W. VEECK, *Die Alamannen in Württemberg*, Berlin and Leipzig, 1931.

W. WEGEWITZ, *Die langobardische Kultur im Gau Moswidi (Niederelbe) zu Beginn unserer Zeitrechnung*, Hildesheim, 1937.

J. WERNER, *Die Langobarden in Pannonien. Beiträge zur Kenntnis der langobardischen Bodenfunde vor 568*, Munich, 1962.

H. ZEISS, *Die Grabfunde aus dem spanischen Westgotenreich*, Berlin and Leipzig, 1934.

H. ZEISS, *Studien zu den Grabfunden aus dem Burgundenreich an der Rhône*, Munich, 1938.

J. ZEMAN, *Severni Morava v mladši dobe rímské* ("Northern Moravia in the later Roman Empire"), Prague, 1961.

L. F. ZOTZ, *Die spätgermanische Kultur Schlesiens im Gräberfeld von Gross-Sürding*, Leipzig, 1935.

Individual Monuments and Groups of Monuments

H. ARBMAN, "Birka, Sveriges äldsta handelsstad", in *Från forntid och Medeltid*, I, Stockholm, 1939.

H. ARBMAN, *Birka*, I, *Die Gräber*, Stockholm, 1940 and 1943.

E. BENINGER, "Der Wandalenfund von Czéke-Cejkov", *Annalen des Naturhistorischen Museums in Wien*, 45, 1931, 184–224.

J. BRANDT, *Das Urnengräberfeld von Preetz in Holstein*, Neumünster, 1960.

G. DIACONU, *Tîrgşor. Necropola din secololele III–IV e.n.*, Bucharest, 1965.

G. EICHHORN, *Der Urnenfriedhof auf der Schanze von Großromstedt*, Leipzig, 1927.

W. GREMPLER, *Der Fund von Sackrau*, Brandenburg and Berlin, 1887.

W. GREMPLER, *Der II. und III. Fund von Sackrau*, Berlin, 1888.

E. GROHNE, *Mahndorf. Frühgeschichte des Bremischen Raums*, Bremen, 1953.

J. J. HATT, "Une tombe barbare du Ve siècle à Hochfelden (Bas-Rhin)", *Gallia*, 23, 1965, 250–256.

G. KÖRNER, *Der Urnenfriedhof von Rebenstorf im Amte Lüchow*, Hildesheim, 1939.

S. LINDQVIST, *Uppsala högar och Ottars högen*, Stockholm, 1936.

B. MITREA and C. PREDA, *Necropole din secolul al IV^{lea} e. n. în Muntenia*, Bucharest, 1966.

J. PETERSEN, *Gravplassen fra Store-Dal i Skjeberg*, Oslo, 1916.

K. RADDATZ, *Das Wagengrab der jüngeren vorrömischen Eisenzeit von Husby, Kr. Flensburg*, Neumünster, 1967.

A. RANGS-BORCHLING, *Das Urnengräberfeld von Hornbek in Holstein*, Neumünster, 1963.

E. SCHULDT, *Pritzier. Ein Urnenfriedhof der späten Römischen Kaiserzeit in Mecklenburg*, Berlin, 1955.

W. SCHULZ, *Das Fürstengrab von Hassleben*, Berlin and Leipzig, 1933.

W. SCHULZ, *Leuna. Ein germanischer Bestattungsplatz der spätrömischen Kaiserzeit*, Berlin, 1953.

B. STJERNQUIST, *Simris. On Cultural Connections of Scania in the Roman Iron Age*, Bonn and Lund, 1955.

Culture, Art and Handicrafts

O. ALMGREN, *Studien über nordeuropäische Fibelformen der ersten nachchristlichen Jahrhunderte mit Berücksichtigung der provinzialrömischen und südrussischen Formen*, Stockholm, 1897, 2nd ed., Leipzig, 1923.

H. ARBMAN, *Schweden und das karolingische Reich*, Stockholm, 1937.

G. ARVIDSSON, *Vendelstile, Email und Glas im 7.–8. Jahrhundert* (Valsgärdestudien, 1), Uppsala, 1941.

J. BØE, *Jernalderens keramikk i Norge*, Bergen, 1921.

H. BOTT, *Bajuwarischer Schmuck der Agilolfingerzeit*, Munich, 1952.

J. BRØNDSTED, *Early English Ornament*, London and Copenhagen, 1924.

S. FUCHS, *Die langobardischen Goldblattkreuze aus der Zone südwärts der Alpen*, Berlin, 1938.

G. GJESSING, "De norske gullbrakteaterne", *Univ. Oldsaksamlings Skrifter*, 2, 1929, 127–176.

G. HASELOFF, *Der Tassilokelch*, Munich, 1951.

W. HOLMQUIST, *Tauschierte Metallarbeiten des Nordens aus Römerzeit und Völkerwanderung*, Stockholm, 1951.

O. KLINDT-JENSEN, "Foreign Influences in Denmark's Early Iron Age", *Acta Archaeologica*, 20, 1949, 1–229.

H. KÜHN, *Die germanischen Bügelfibeln der Rheinprovinz*, Bonn, 1940.

S. LINDQVIST, *Vendelkulturens ålder och ursprung*, Stockholm, 1926.

S. LINDQVIST, *Gotlands Bildsteine*, I–II, Stockholm, 1941.

M. B. MACKEPRANG, *De nordiske gullbrakteater*, Århus, 1952.

E. MEYER, "Die Bügelknopffibel", *Arbeits- und Forschungsberichte zur Sächsischen Bodendenkmalpflege*, 8, 1960, 216–349.

A. ODOBESCO, *Le trésor de Pétrossa*, I–III, Paris, 1899–1900.

M. ØRSNES, *Form og stil i Sydskandinaviens yngre germanske jernalder*, Copenhagen, 1966.

P. PAULSEN, *Studien zur Wikinger-Kultur*, Neumünster, 1933.

K. RADDATZ, *Der Thorsberger Moorfund. Gürtelteile und Körperschmuck*, Neumünster, 1957.

B. SALIN, *Die germanische Tierornamentik*, Stockholm, 1904.

E. SALIN, *La civilisation mérovingienne*, I–IV, Paris, 1950–1959.

S. THOMAS, "Studien zu den germanischen Kämmen der Kaiserzeit", *Arbeits- und Forschungsberichte zur Sächsischen Bodendenkmalpflege*, 8, 1960, 54–215.

K. WEIDEMANN, "Zur Interpretation einiger kaiserzeitlicher Urnenfriedhöfe in Nordwestdeutschland", *Jahrbuch des Römisch-Germanischen Zentralmuseums*, 12, 1965, 84–92.

J. WERNER, *Die beiden Zierscheiben des Thorsberger Moorfundes. Ein Beitrag zur frühgermanischen Kunst- und Religionsgeschichte*, Berlin and Leipzig, 1941.

J. WERNER, "Zur Entstehung der Reihengräberzivilisation", *Archaeologia geogr.*, 1, 1950, 23–32.

J. WERNER, *Das Aufkommen von Bild und Schrift in Nordeuropa*, Munich, 1966.

H. WILLERS, *Die römische Bronzeeimer von Hemmoor*, Hannover and Leipzig, 1901.

H. WILLERS, *Neue Untersuchungen über die römische Bronzeindustrie von Capua und von Niedergermanien, insbesondere auf die Funde aus Deutschland und dem Norden hin*, Hannover and Leipzig, 1907.

Religion

C. J. BECKER, "Die zeitliche Stellung des Hjortspring-Fundes innerhalb der vorrömischen Eisenzeit in Dänemark", *Acta Archaeologica*, 19, 1948, 145–187.

C. ENGELHARDT, *Thorsbjerg Mosefund*, Copenhagen, 1863.

C. ENGELHARDT, *Nydam Mosefund 1859–63*, Copenhagen, 1865.

C. ENGELHARDT, *Kragehulmosefund*, Copenhagen, 1867.

C. ENGELHARDT, *Vimose Fundet*, Copenhagen, 1896.

H. GEISSLINGER, *Horte als Geschichtsquelle, dargestellt an den völkerwanderungs- und merovingerzeitlichen Funden des südwestlichen Ostseeraums*, Neumünster, 1967.

S. GRIEG, "Vikingertidens Skattefund", *Univ. Oldsaksamlings Skrifter*, 2, 1929, 177–312.

W. GRØNBECH, *Kultur und Religion der Germanen*, I–II, 2nd ed., Hamburg, 1939.

H. HAYEN, "Menschenförmige Holzfiguren an einem Bohlweg des dritten Jahrhunderts v.Chr. Geb.", *Nachrichten aus Niedersachsens Urgeschichte*, 35, 1966, 138–140.

U. E. HAGBERG, *The Archaeology of Skedemosse*, I–II, Stockholm, 1967.

A. OLDEBERG, "Några träidoler från förhistorisk och senare tid", *Fornvännen*, 52, 1957, 247–258.

G. ROSENBERG, "Hjortspringfundet", *Nordiske Fortidsminder*, III, 1, Copenhagen, 1937.

M. STENBERGER, *Die Schatzfunde Gotlands der Wikingerzeit*, Stockholm, 1958.

T. SULIMIRSKI, "The Hoard of Zamość", *Archaeologia Polski*, 11, 1966, 118–173.

Settlements, Economy and Technology

C. J. BECKER, "Ein früheisenzeitliches Dorf bei Grøntoft, Westjütland", *Acta Archaeologica*, 36, 1965, 209–222.

A. W. BRØGGER, *Winlandfahrten. Wikinger entdecken Amerika*, Hamburg, 1939.

O. DOPPELFELD, G. BEHM and O. F. GANDERT, "Das germanische Dorf auf dem Bärhorst bei Nauen", *Prähistorische Zeitschrift*, 28/29, 1937/38, 284–337.

H. J. EGGERS, *Der römische Import im Freien Germanien*, Hamburg, 1951.

P. FRIIS and P. L. JENSEN, "En jernalderhustomt med kaelder på Grøn-hedens mark", *Kuml*, 1966/67, 31–58.

F. GENZMER, *Germanische Seefahrt und Seegeltung*, Munich, 1944.

P. V. GLOB, *Ard og Plov i Nordens Oldtid*, Århus, 1951.

G. HATT, *The Ownership of Cultivated Land*, Copenhagen, 1939.

G. HATT, *Nørre Fjand. An Early Iron-Age Village Site in West Jutland*, Copenhagen, 1957.

B. HOUGEN, *Fra seter til gård*, Oslo, 1947.

H. JANKUHN, *Haithabu. Ein Handelsplatz der Wikingerzeit*, 3rd ed., Neu-münster, 1956.

K. JANKUHN, "Ackerfluren der Eisenzeit und ihre Bedeutung für die frühere Wirtschaftsgeschichte", *37.–38. Bericht der Römisch-Germani-schen Kommission 1956/57*, 1958, 148–214.

G. KOSSACK, "Zur Frage der Dauer germanischer Siedlungen in der römi-schen Kaiserzeit", *Zeitschrift für Schleswig-Holsteinische Geschichte*, 91, 1966, 13–42.

J. N. L. MYRES, *Anglo-Saxon Pottery and the Settlement of England*, Ox-ford, 1969.

H. OHLHAVER, *Der germanische Schmied und sein Werkzeug*, Leipzig, 1939.

R. PLEINER, "Die Eisengewinnung in der 'Germania Magna' zur römi-schen Kaiserzeit", *45. Bericht der Römisch-Germanischen Kommission*, 1964, 11–86.

M. STENBERGER (ed.), *Fortida gårdar i Island*, Copenhagen, 1943.

M. STENBERGER (ed.), *Vallhagar. A Migration Period Settlement on Gotland, Sweden*, I–II, Stockholm, 1955.

J. WERNER, "Fernhandel und Naturalwirtschaft im östlichen Merovinger-reich nach archäologischen und numismatischen Zeugnissen", *42. Bericht der Römisch-Germanischen Kommission 1961*, 1962, 307–346.

J. WERNER, *Waage und Geld in der Merovingerzeit*, Munich, 1954.

Social Structure

K. von AMIRA, *Grundriss des germanischen Rechts*, Strasbourg, 1913.

H. J. EGGERS, "Lübsow, ein germanischer Fürstensitz der älteren Kaiser-zeit", *Prähistorische Zeitschrift*, 34/35, 1949/50, 58–111.

S. C. HAWKES and G. C. DUNNING, "Krieger und Siedler in Britannien während des 4. und 5. Jahrhunderts", *43.–44. Bericht der Römisch-Germanischen Kommission 162/63*, 1964, 155–231.

M. JAHN, *Die Bewaffnung der Germanen in der ältesten Eisenzeit etwa von 700 v.Chr. bis 200 n.Chr.*, Würzburg, 1916.

M. JAHN, *Der Reitersporn, seine Entstehung und früheste Entwicklung*, Leipzig, 1921.

H. JANKUHN, *Die Wehranlagen der Wikingerzeit zwischen Schlei und Treene*, Neumünster, 1937.

A. KIEKEBUSCH, "Ein germanisches Reitergrab der späten Völkerwan-derungszeit von Neukölln (Rixdorf) bei Berlin", *Prähistorische Zeit-schrift*, 4, 1912, 395–403.

V. ONDROUCH, *Bohaté Hroby z Doby Rímskej na Slovensku*, Bratislava, 1957.

K. RADDATZ, "Römische Äxte aus dem Freien Germanien", *Offa*, 17/18, 1959/61, 17–25.

K. RADDATZ, "Ringknaufschwerter aus germanischen Kriegergräbern", *Offa*, 17/18, 1959/61, 26–56.

K. RADDATZ, "Pfeilspitzen aus dem Moorfund von Nydam", *Offa*, 20, 1963, 49–56.

K. RADDATZ, *Die Bewaffnung der Germanen in der jüngeren römischen Kaiserzeit*, Göttingen, 1967.

H. ROOSENS, "Laeti, Foederati und andere spätrömische Bevölkerungsniederschläge im belgischen Raum", *Die Kunde*, new series, 18, 1967, 89–109.

F. STEIN, *Adelsgräber des achten Jahrhunderts in Deutschland*, Berlin, 1967.

M. STENBERGER, "Eketorp's Borg, a Fortified Village in Öland", *Acta Archaeologica*, 38, 1966, 203–214.

K. W. STRUVE, "Die Moorleiche von Dätgen. Ein Diskussionsbeitrag zur Strafopferthese", *Offa*, 24, 1967, 33–76.

J. WERNER, "Die römischen Bronzegeschirrdepots des 3. Jahrhunderts und die mitteldeutsche Skelettgräbergruppe", *Marburger Studien*, Darmstadt, 1938, 259–267.

J. WERNER, *Das Alamannische Fürstengrab von Wittislingen*, Munich, 1950.

LIST OF ILLUSTRATIONS

10   *Votive deposit of two wooden ceremonial wagons with rich bronze fittings. From bog at Dejbjerg, Ringkøbing district, Denmark. Of Celtic workmanship, exported and used for Germanic cult purposes. 1st c. B.C. National Museum, Copenhagen. (Ph. Museum).*

11   *Bronze fitting from the first of the Dejbjerg wagons. (After H. Petersen).*

12   *Wooden shields from bog at Hjortspring, Sønderborg district, Denmark. About 100 B.C. National Museum, Copenhagen. (Ph. Museum).*

13   *Fragments of boat from bog at Hjortspring, as discovered. (Ph. National Museum, Copenhagen).*

14   *Model of Hjortspring boat. (Ph. National Museum, Copenhagen).*

15   *Plank road in bog at Stapel, Lower Saxony, Germany. About beginning of 1st c. A.D. (Ph. Museum für Naturkunde und Vorgeschichte, Oldenburg i.O.).*

16   *Anthropomorphic wooden figure (female) found beside a plank road in bog at Hude, Lower Saxony, Germany. About beginning of 1st c. A.D. Museum für Naturgeschichte und Vorgeschichte, Oldenburg i.O. (Ph. Museum).*

17   *The same: male figure.*

18   *Bronze collar in the form of a crown: votive offering from a bog near Emmendorf, Lower Saxony, Germony. 3rd c. B.C. Niedersächsisches Landesmuseum, Hannover. (Ph. Museum).*

19   *Bronze cauldron with silver panels from a bog at Gundestrup, Ålborg district, Denmark. Of Celtic workmanship, used for Germanic cult purposes. 1st c. B.C. National Museum, Copenhagen. (Ph. Museum).*

20   *Representation of hunting scene on jar from Kraghede (Plate 21).*
        (After S. Müller).

21   *Jar from cremation burial at Kraghede, Hjørring district, Denmark.*
        End of 1st c. B.C. National Museum, Copenhagen. (Ph. Museum).

22   *Pottery vessels from cremation burial near Haldern, Lower Rhine-*
        land, Germany. 1st c. B.C. Rheinisches Landesmuseum, Bonn.
        (Ph. Museum).

23   *The same.*

24–25   *Pottery vessel with decoration of meanders and figures of horses,*
        from cremation burial at Hohenferchesar, Brandenburg, Germany.
        1st c. A.D. Genthin Museum. (Ph. Museum).

26   *Cinerary urn from tomb at Planany, near Kolin, Czechoslovakia.*
        About beginning of 1st c. A.D. Kolin Museum. (After J. Poulik).

27   *Bronze cup with handle in the form of a horse (very probably of*
        Celtic workmanship) from tomb at Mollerup, Viborg district,
        Denmark. About beginning of 1st c. A.D. National Museum,
        Copenhagen. (Ph. Museum).

28   *Bronze belt catch from cremation burial at Haldern, Lower Rhine-*
        land, Germany. 1st c. B.C. Rheinisches Landesmuseum, Bonn.
        (Ph. Museum).

29–32   *Fibulas of cast bronze. End of 1s c. B.C. Denmark. No. 29 from*
        Skørping, Ålborg district. No. 30 from Lindering Kær, Hjørring
        district. No. 31 from Åborg district. No. 32: provenance unknown.
        National Museum, Copenhagen. (Ph. Museum).

33   *Belt made of decorated bronze plaques, from cremation burial at*
        Harmstorf, Schleswig-Holstein, Germany. 1st c. B.C. Schleswig-
        Holsteinisches Landesmuseum für Vor- und Frühgeschichte,
        Schleswig. (Ph. Museum).

46–47   *Votive deposit from tomb No. 403 in cremation cemetery at Ham-felde, Schleswig-Holstein, Germany. It consists of a pottery cine-rary urn (No. 46), a Roman sword with ring pommel and chape, two lance heads, shield mountings and two spurs (No. 47). About 200 A.D. Schleswig-Holsteinisches Landesmuseum für Vor- und Frühgeschichte, Schleswig. (Ph. Museum).*

48   *Hoard found near Hede, Västmanland, Sweden, consisting of a gold bracelet and three biconical beads. 2nd c. A.D. Statens Historiska Museum, Stockholm. (Ph. Museum).*

49   *Rich votive deposit of bronze, silver and gold ornaments found near Vester Mellerup, Hjørring district, Denmark. About 100 A.D. National Museum, Copenhagen. (Ph. Museum).*

50   *Inhumation tomb with rich grave goods (pottery vessels). From Buldbjerg, Århus district, Denmark. About 100 A.D. National Museum, Copenhagen. (Ph. Museum).*

51   *Detail of fibula in form of a boar, from the Brodelbrunnen ("Bub-bling Well"), Bad Pyrmont, Westphalia, Germany. 2nd–3rd c. A.D. Bad Pyrmont Museum. (Ph. Museum).*

52   *Roman bronze vessel and specimens of the 250 Germanic and Roman fibulas and silver coins of Domitian, Trajan and Caracalla deposited in the Brodelbrunnen, Bad Pyrmont. 2nd–3rd c. A.D. Bad Pyrmont Museum. (Ph. Museum).*

53   *Bronze figure with runic inscription found in the cremation tomb of a warrior. The other grave goods included a bronze cauldron, an iron sword, two lances, a spear and shield mountings. From Frøyhov, Akershus, Norway. 3rd c. A.D. Universitetets Oldsak-samling, Oslo. (Ph. Museum).*

54–55   *Silver gilt cup from a rich tomb near Himlingøje, Præstø district, Denmark. 3rd c. A.D. National Museum, Copenhagen (Ph. Museum).*

56   *Brass figure of bovid from Berlin-Schöneberg. 3rd c. A.D. Former Staatliches Museum für Vor- und Frühgeschichte, Berlin. (Ph. Museum).*

57   *Pottery vessel from cremation cemetery at Kostelec na Hané, Moravia, Czechoslovakia. 3rd c. A.D. Olomouc Museum. (After J. Poulik).*

58   *Silver fibula with silver gilt rosette and runic inscription on catch-plate, from a richly furnished woman's tomb at Værløse, Copenhagen. (Ph. Museum).*

59   *Iron lance head with runic inscriptions and magical signs inlaid in silver, from Dahmsdorf, Brandenburg, Germany. 3rd c. A.D. Müncheberg Museum. (After W. Krause).*

60–63   *Iron lance head with magical signs inlaid in silver (Nos. 60, 61) and a Roman iron sword with two figures (Mars and Victory) inlaid in copper (Nos. 62, 63), from the tomb of a Vandal warrior at Podlodow, Tomaszów Lubelski district, Poland. 3rd c. A.D. Lublin Museum. (Ph. Museum).*

64   *Plan of Germanic village on Bärhorst, near Nauen, Brandenburg, Germany. 3rd c. A.D. (After O. Doppelfeld and G. Behm).*

65   *Votive deposit found in bog at Thorsberg, Schleswig-Holstein, Germany: ornamental plaque. Roman provincial workmanship, with parts added by a Germanic craftsman. 3rd c. A.D. Schleswig-Holsteinisches Landesmuseum für Vor- und Frühgeschichte, Schleswig. (Ph. Museum).*

66–68   *The same: bronze circlet (Germanic workmanship).*

69   *The same: ornamental plaque (Roman provincial work, with parts added by a Germanic craftsman).*

70   *The same: horse trappings.*

71   *Gold fibula decorated with granulation, from the princely tomb at Straže, Slovakia. Beginning of 4th c. A.D. Piešt'any Museum. (Ph. Museum).*

72   *Votive deposit found in bog at Thorsberg, Schleswig Holstein, Germany: bit. 3rd c. A.D. Schleswig-Holsteinisches Landesmuseum für Vor- und Frühgeschichte, Schleswig. (Ph. Museum).*

73   *Gold fibula decorated with granulation, from the princely tomb at Straže, Slovakia. Beginning of 4th c. A.D. Piešt'any Museum. (Ph. Museum).*

74   *Grave goods from woman's tomb at Skyttemarksvej, Præstø district, Denmark: glass and amber beads, spirals of silver and bronze wire. 3rd–4th c. A.D. National Museum, Copenhagen. (Ph. Museum).*

75   *The same: swastika fibula in silver gilt, five bucket-shaped trinkets in silver and five in bronze, a needle and two silver capsules.*

76   *Bowl with moulded decoration (Roman provincial work) and pedestal cup (Germanic work) from the princely tomb at Czéke, Slovakia. Beginning of 4th c. A.D. Kunsthistorisches Museum, Vienna. (Ph. Museum).*

77–78   *Pottery vessel with figured decoration from cremation cemetery at Borgstedt, Schleswig-Holstein, Germany. 4th c. A.D. Schleswig-Holsteinisches Landesmuseum für Vor- und Frühgeschichte, Schleswig. (Ph. Museum).*

79–80   *The same: detail of decoration.*

81   *Pottery vessel decorated with human figures, from Brno-Obrany, Moravia. 4th c. A.D. Brno Museum. (Ph. Museum).*

82–83   *Votive deposit of some 100 miniature boats in gold foil contained in a pottery vessel, found at Nors, Thisted district, Denmark. Probably 2nd–4th c. A.D. National Museum, Copenhagen. (Ph. Museum).*

84   *Pottery vessels from a horseman's tomb (No. 2, 1926) at Leuna, Saxony, Germany. Beginning of 4th c. A.D. Landesmuseum für Vorgeschichte, Halle. (Ph. Museum).*

85   *Animal's head in carved wood from the sacred bog of Vimose, Odense district, Denmark. About 300 A.D. National Museum, Copenhagen. (Ph. Museum).*

86   *Gold rings from place of sacrifice in Skedemosse bog, Öland, Sweden. 3rd–4th c. A.D. Statens Historiska Museum, Stockholm. (Ph. Museum).*

87   *The same.*

88   *Silver disc fibula with gilt ornamental plaque from Tangendorf, Lower Saxony, Germany. 3rd–4th c. A.D. Helms Museum, Hamburg–Harburg. (Ph. Museum).*

89   *Wooden figure of a bearded god found near a pile of stones in a bog at Broddenbjerg, Viborg district, Denmark, together with broken pottery vessels. 1st–5th c. A.D. National Museum, Copenhagen. (Ph. Museum).*

90   *Phallic figures of a bearded god found in a bog at Njutanger, Hälsingland, Sweden. 1st–5th c. A.D. Statens Historiska Museum, Stockholm. (Ph. Museum).*

91   *The same: detail of head.*

92–95   *Wooden figures of a man and a woman found in a bog at Braak, Schleswig-Holstein, Germany. About 5th c. A.D. Schleswig-Holsteinisches Landesmuseum für Vor- und Frühgeschichte, Schleswig. (Ph. Museum).*

96   *Oar-propelled boat from the Nydam bog, Åbenrå district, Denmark. 4th c. A.D. Schleswig-Holsteinisches Landesmuseum für Vor- und Frühgeschichte, Schleswig. (Ph. Museum).*

97   *Decoration of gold horn with runic inscriptions found at Gallehus, Tønder district, Denmark, in 1734. Beginning of 5th c. A.D.*

98   *One of the two Gallehus horns: drawings of 1734 (left) and 1736 (right). The horns were stolen in 1802 and melted down.*

99   *Head of a man found in a bog at Osterby, Schleswig-Holstein, Germany. The head had been struck off the body and laid in the bog under a fur cape. It is dated to the early centuries of the Christian era. The hair style is similar to that of the Suebi as described by Tacitus. Schleswig-Holsteinisches Landesmuseum für Vor- und Frühgeschichte, Schleswig. (Ph. Museum).*

100   *Casket of yew wood with a runic inscription from the Garbolle bog, Sørø district, Denmark. About 400 A.D. National Museum, Copenhagen. (Ph. Museum).*

101   *Silver fibula, inlaid with gold and niello, from a warrior's tomb at Vermand, Aisne, France. Roman provincial work; the tomb, however, did not belong to a Roman, but probably to a Frank. 4th c. A.D. Metropolitan Museum, New York. (Ph. Museum).*

102   *Silver plaque, inlaid with gold and niello, decorating the shaft of a ceremonial lance, from the same tomb.*

103   *Fibula of silver foil from a tomb at Kvarnløse, Holbæk district, Denmark. Beginning of 5th c. A.D. National Museum, Copenhagen. (Ph. Museum).*

104   *Swastika fibula found in Denmark. 4th–5th c. A.D. National Museum, Copenhagen. (Ph. Museum).*

105   *The same.*

106   *The same.*

107   *Hoard consisting of a gold fibula, two gold bracelets, three finger rings, four small bell-shaped buttons, a spiral ring and a coin of Constantine II (337–340): part of a larger hoard found under a large stone at Lengerich, East Friesland, Germany. Two other considerable hoards were found under stones in the immediate vicinity. End of 4th c. A.D. Niedersächsisches Landesmuseum, Hannover. (Ph. Museum).*

108   *Two fibulas of silver leaf, gilded, two fibulas of silver leaf, a silver needle with an axe-shaped head and a bronze needle, from tombs found near Wiesbaden, Hesse, Germany. 5th c. A.D. Nassauisches Landesmuseum, Wiesbaden. (Ph. Museum).*

109   *Bronze belt buckle with traces of gilding, found in a tomb at Košice, Slovakia, together with a metal mirror and a bone comb. Košice Museum. (Ph. Museum).*

110   *First Szilagysomlyo hoard, found at Szilagysomlyo (Şimleul Silvaniei), Transylvania, Rumania, in 1797: gold pendant with double eyelet and belt ornament decorated with human figures in repoussé* (Presstechnik). *About 400 A.D. Kunsthistorisches Museum, Vienna. (Ph. Museum).*

111   *The same: gold chain with trinkets representing miniature tools.*

112–i16 *The same: gold medallions of the Emperors Constantius II (337–361), Valens (364–378) and Gratian (367–383).*

117   *Tomb of a princess at Hochfelden, Alsace: necklace of plaited gold wire. 5th c. A.D. Musée de Rohan, Strasbourg. (Ph. G. Bertin).*

118   *The same: two fibulas in silver leaf and a metal mirror.*

119   *The same: two gold ear-rings and twenty decorative pieces in gold foil.*

120   *Necklace of plaited gold wire, nine gold pendants and a round capsule with eyelets (probably the remains of another necklace) found in a princess's tomb at Nasobrky, Moravia, Czechoslovakia. 6th c. A.D. Kunsthistorisches Museum, Vienna. (Ph. Museum).*

121   *Princely tomb at Wolfsheim, Rhineland-Palatinate, Germany, with rich grave goods: gold necklace and pectoral of Iranian origin, gold fibula, gold bracelet and three buckles, amber pendant from sword and a coin of Valentinian (364–375). 5th c. A.D. Nassauisches Landesmuseum, Wiesbaden. (Ph. Museum).*

122   *Gold bracelets with catches in the shape of animals' heads, from a tomb at Puszta Bakod, Pest, Hungary. 5th c. A.D. Magyar Nemzeti Muzeum, Budapest. (Ph. Museum).*

123   *Necklace of plaited gold wire and gold necklace with studs of almandine and crescent-shaped and heart-shaped pendants, from a tomb at Puszta Bakod, Pest, Hungary. 5th c. A.D. Magyar Nemzeti Muzeum, Budapest. (Ph. Museum).*

124   *Hoard found in a pottery jar at Dortmund, Germany, consisting of three gold necklaces and 444 Roman gold coins. 5th c. A.D. Städtisches Museum, Dortmund. (Ph. Museum).*

125   *Tomb of King Childeric (d. 482), near Tournai, Belgium, with valuable grave goods, discovered in 1653: gold cicadas, originally on a fur cape. Cabinet des Médailles, Bibliothèque Nationale, Paris. (Ph. Cabinet des Médailles).*

126   *The same: signet ring with the inscription "Childerici Regis", by which the tomb was identified.*

127   *The same: decoration on hilt of a long sword.*

128   *The same: decoration on fragments of hilt and scabbard of a short sword.*

129   *The same: hilt of the long sword (on right) and fragments of hilt and scabbard of the short sword (on left).*

130   *Decorative fibula from Rebrény, Slovakia. About 400 A.D. Kunsthistorisches Museum, Vienna. (Ph. Museum).*

131   *Fibula with arms of equal length and two falcon fibulas (of Saxon workmanship)—all gilded—from a tomb at Anderlingen, Lower Saxony, Germany. 5th c. A.D. Niedersächsisches Landesmuseum, Hannover. (Ph. Museum).*

132   *Fibula of gilt bronze from 5th c. woman's tomb at Omundrød, Vestfold, Norway. End of 5th c. A.D. Universitetets Oldsaksamling, Oslo. (Ph. Museum).*

133   *The same.*

134   *Part of the rich grave furniture of the 5th c. woman's tomb at Omundrød: two pottery vessels, two glass vessels, the two gilt bronze fibulas, two cross-shaped fibulas, various pieces of ornament and weaving implements. End of 5th c. A.D. Universitetets Oldsaksamling, Oslo. (Ph. Museum).*

135   *Pendant from a necklace. From a hoard found at Cesena, Forlì province, Italy. About 500 A.D. Metropolitan Museum, New York. (Ph. Museum).*

136–137 *Bronze fibulas in the form of a falcon. Probably from a tomb in northern France. 6th–7th c. A.D. Metropolitan Museum, New York. (Ph. Museum).*

138   *Two gilt bronze fibulas in the form of a falcon. Probably from a tomb in northern France. 6th c. A.D. Metropolitan Museum, New York. (Ph. Museum).*

139   *Fibula in the form of an eagle, in cloisonné enamel. Hoard found at Cesena, Forlì province, Italy. About 500 A.D. Germanisches Nationalmuseum, Nuremberg. (Ph. Museum).*

140   *Two fibulas in the form of an eagle, cloisonné enamel (Ostrogothic work). Found along with a silver buckle in a tomb on the Via Flaminia, near Rome. Beginning of 6th c. A.D. Capitoline Museum, Rome. (Ph. Museum).*

141   *Bronze fibula in the form of a bird (Visigothic work), found at Calatayud, Zaragoza province, Spain. After 500 A.D. Museo Arqueológico Nacional, Madrid. (Ph. Museum).*

142   *Two bronze fibulas from a 6th c. Frankish tomb in northern France. Metropolitan Museum, New York. (Ph. Museum).*

143   *Two fibulas and a bronze buckle (Ostrogothic work) from a tomb in Romagna, Italy. 6th c. A.D. Germanisches Nationalmuseum, Nuremberg. (Ph. Museum).*

144   *Two silver gilt fibulas from a late 6th c. Frankish tomb in northern France. Metropolitan Museum, New York. (Ph. Museum).*

145   *The Ostrogothic queen Amalasuntha (d. 535). Ivory diptych. 6th c. A.D. Kunsthistorisches Museum, Vienna. (Ph. Museum).*

146   *Coin of the Vandal king Gunthamund (d. 496), found in Tunisia. Cabinet des Médailles, Bibliothèque Nationale, Paris. (Ph. Cabinet des Médailles).*

147   *The same.*

148 *Hoard found at Gourdon, Lot, France: paten inlaid with almandines. The hoard is generally thought to have belonged to the Burgundian king Sigismund (d. 524). Cabinet des Médailles, Bibliothèque Nationale, Paris. (Ph. Cabinet des Médailles).*

149 *The same: chased gold cup.*

150 *Belt ornaments, inlaid with silver, from a tomb at Werghoffen, Alsace. 7th c. A.D. Musée de Rohan, Strasbourg. (Ph. G. Bertin).*

151 *Silver disc fibula mounted with precious stones, from a tomb at Werghoffen, Alsace. 7th c. A.D. Musée de Rohan, Strasbourg. (Ph. G. Bertin).*

152 *The same.*

153 *Bronze jug and pan from a horseman's tomb at Ittenheim, Alsace. 7th c. A.D. Musée de Rohan, Strasbourg. (Ph. G. Bertin).*

154 *Three silver phaleras from a horseman's tomb at Ittenheim, Alsace. 7th c. A.D. Musée de Rohan, Strasbourg. (Ph. G. Bertin).*

155 *Carolingian sword found in Strasbourg (Kalbsgasse 5). Musée de Rohan, Strasbourg. (Ph. G. Bertin).*

156 *Silver gilt ear-rings from a tomb at Molsheim, Alsace. 7th c. A.D. Musée de Rohan, Strasbourg. (Ph. G. Bertin).*

157 *Helmet with chin-piece from a warrior's tomb at Baldenheim, Alsace. The tomb can be dated to about 600 A.D.; the helmet (perhaps an heirloom) is 6th c. Musée de Rohan, Strasbourg. (Ph. G. Bertin).*

INDEX

THE TEXT AND ILLUSTRATIONS IN THIS VOLUME
WERE PRINTED ON THE PRESSES OF
NAGEL PUBLISHERS IN GENEVA

FINISHED IN AUGUST 1971
BINDING BY NAGEL PUBLISHERS, GENEVA

OFFSET COLOUR SEPARATIONS BY
PHOTOLITHOS ARGRAF, GENEVA

LEGAL DEPOSIT No 540

PRINTED IN SWITZERLAND

Printed in Switzerland